風
水

THE
FENG
SHUI
DOCTOR

風水

THE FENG SHUI DOCTOR

ANCIENT SKILLS FOR MODERN LIVING

PAUL DARBY

FOREWORD BY MARTIN SHAW

DUNCAN BAIRD PUBLISHERS

LONDON

THE FENG SHUI DOCTOR
PAUL DARBY

To Annie, Tiger Lady, "the wind beneath my wings", my hero – T.M.D. – and to a bundle of sparkle called Keira Marie, who has added new joy to my world!

Distributed in the USA and Canada by Sterling Publishing Co., Inc.
387 Park Avenue South
New York, NY 10016-8810

This edition first published in the UK and USA in 2007 by
Duncan Baird Publishers Ltd
Sixth Floor, Castle House
75–76 Wells Street
London W1T 3QH

Managing Editor: Kelly Thompson
Editor: Katie John
Managing Designer: Daniel Sturges
Designer: Justin Ford
Commissioned Calligraphy: Yukki Yaura

Library of Congress Cataloging-in-Publication Data Available

ISBN-13: 978-1-84483-398-6
ISBN-10: 1-84483-398-4

10 9 8 7 6 5 4 3 2 1

Typeset in Gill Sans
Color reproduction by Colourscan, Singapore
Printed in Singapore

For information about custom editions, special sales, premium and corporate purchases, please contact Sterling Special Sales Department at 800-805-5489 or specialsales@sterlingpub.com.

Publisher's note

The publishers and author cannot accept any responsibility for any injuries or damage incurred as a result of using any of the therapeutic methods described or mentioned in this book.

CONTENTS

FOREWORD

By Martin Shaw

An award-winning actor, Martin Shaw has played leading roles in many productions in the West End, such as Man For All Seasons *and* Are You Lonesome Tonight, *as well as on Broadway. He has also starred in numerous British TV programmes, including* Judge John Deed, Always and Everyone *and* The Professionals.

I had been interested in subtle energy and mysticism for years when I discovered the art of feng shui. It had become clear to me that a lot of our supposed progress was actually insulating us from the treasure trove of ancient knowledge that informs feng shui. The scepticism of many people regarding subtle energy had kept us in the dark for too long. Nowadays, however, I am delighted to say that the profound truths of this knowledge are coming into our lives more and more.

Feng shui came into my own life out of an intuitive sense that there was something more to the "feeling" of a place than simply physical beauty or the artful placement of objects and furniture. It struck me that some places immediately conveyed a sense of peace and tranquillity, while others exuded chaos and discomfort.

Some years ago, I had a long period out of work. Money was tight, and I was also owed money. I bought a basic feng shui book and found that the money and career areas of the cottage in which I lived were, in terms of feng shui, terrible. I made adjustments according to the book's suggestions and waited. Then, three days later, the money I was owed came in; and the job offers followed soon after. So, when I saw feng shui consultant Paul Darby on daytime TV show *Richard and Judy*, a seed had already been sown. However, it was Paul's vibrant personality and utter conviction in his art that led me to ask him for a home visit and a consultation.

My home, an old Quaker Meeting House, was full of energies, memories and influences. Paul spent hours working through the house, his deep knowledge and formidable intuition identifying the changes that I needed, and mapping the journey I was about to undertake. This involved some redecorating, as well as repositioning various objects. The immediate results were gratifying in terms of the house's look and feel, yet there also followed a deeper and more gradual adjustment of my life within and beyond my home. Now, few visitors fail to comment on the peaceful and positive atmosphere of my home, and I myself have an ongoing and deeply satisfying sense of my own and the house's energies coming into balance.

Paul and his wife Annie have become firm and faithful friends. Paul's scholarship and Ph.D speak for themselves, but 10 minutes in his company will show you what a remarkable human being he is. His positivity and joyful participation in life quickly bring you to laughter and a sense of lightness and trust. Paul's vast knowledge and advice are ceaselessly valuable. He is a force of nature, and I hope that this book takes you on a fascinating and rewarding journey, bringing you peace and harmony. Feng shui is a sea of wisdom and knowledge. Dive in!

Martin Shaw

INTRODUCTION

Yet another book on feng shui – but this one isn't for your coffee table or your bookshelves. It's written to be useful, not ornamental, and designed for you to keep handy, to carry in your bag or to use at a DIY or home improvement store.

Feng shui is a traditional Chinese art dating back thousands of years, but it can be easily adapted for the 21st century. This book sheds light on the underlying beliefs and practices, to give you a feel for feng shui. It also shows you how you can use these ancient skills in a practical way as a guide for your everyday life.

The basis of feng shui

The words *feng shui* literally mean "wind" and "water". They refer to the flowing motion of chi, the energy that exists throughout the universe. Feng shui, pronounced "fung schway" (or "fong choy"), involves assessing and adjusting the energies in each part of your environment – landscape, light, colour, spaces, objects – in order to enhance the flow of chi around and within you. Everything in your world affects you. In turn, you act on the energies in your surroundings, and you can even change those energies consciously.

What feng shui is – and what it isn't

Some people ask me if feng shui is just about moving furniture around, to which I reply flippantly, "No – that's another 'ancient mystical Chinese remedy' called 'the removal van'!" Feng shui is, however, very much about using well-thought-out arrangements of spaces and objects to produce a flow of natural energy that feels right.

How feng shui fits into your life

In traditional Chinese belief, feng shui was seen as one of five aspects of a good life. These aspects are usually given, in order of precedence, as: destiny, luck, feng shui, virtue and knowledge.

Destiny (or karma) is the fate that awaits you in this lifetime as a result of your good or bad deeds in previous lives. Luck, or merit, is the good or bad fortune that you attract with your actions in this life. Feng shui is the way in which you interact with your physical and spiritual environment. Virtue and knowledge are the personal qualities that you can use to bring about your own success.

FIVE ASPECTS OF A GOOD LIFE

First is destiny (Karma)

Second is luck (Merit)

Third is feng shui (Surroundings)

Fourth is virtue (Character)

Fifth is knowledge (Skill, experience)

In this way of thinking, you don't have total control of your life, but you're not a helpless pawn of fate either. You're influenced by your inheritance and environment, but you can still build on your strengths and work on your weaknesses to improve your circumstances. By enabling you to understand and alter your surroundings, feng shui is one method that you can use to change your life for the better.

Traditional wisdom

Centuries ago, the Eastern masters who practised feng shui worked out the ways in which energy, called chi, flowed through the universe. Using devices such as the pa kua (see page 140), a template showing the energies at each compass point, they could channel the chi and enhance people's career, health, wealth and relationships. Their teachings, reinterpreted for the modern world, form the basis of this book. Chapter One outlines how the masters' ideas developed over time. Chapter Two describes the patterns that they identified in all objects and spaces.

By applying feng shui, you'll be "restoring the celestial amidst the mundane", as the ancient masters used to say. They also described the practice of feng shui as "taking out the excess and riding on the phoenix" – the phoenix being the bird that symbolized success and completion.

The universe and ourselves

The fundamental premise in feng shui is that we live within a whirling mass of vibrating energy, which forms patterns that connect the universe in a great "cosmic dance". The chi is pulsating in endless rhythms of creation and destruction, which the feng shui masters called "becoming and unbecoming". This idea is echoed in science today.

In quantum physics, it's suggested that objects, including our bodies, are not solid, but are revolving masses of charged particles, which constantly interact with the particles of their surroundings. Einstein spoke of this activity as a "trembling motion" or a "jiggling" energy. Another physicist said, "Every time you use a toaster, the energy field around it changes its vibrations slightly . . . throughout your close environment." We vibrate like tuning forks, and so does everything else, in a harmonic pattern of electromagnetic flow.

Sensing vibrations

At the individual level, you sense your world through vibrations. The most obvious forms of vibration are light and sound; a more subtle form is electromagnetic energy. You then generate positive or negative feelings in response to these vibrations.

You've probably noticed these effects yourself. For example, do you have favourite pieces of music that make you feel happy or relaxed? Do you have a colour that you always wear to interviews, or for relaxing or flirting? Do certain houses or rooms feel especially welcoming to you, or make you feel uncomfortable?

Restoring the balance of energies

During the past few centuries of civilization, humans have distorted the natural flow of chi in many ways. We've polluted the air with fumes from cars and power stations, discharged chemicals into rivers and created harmful radiation with electricity networks and cellphone masts. This damage leads to a stressful state that the ancient masters called "leaking vitality".

However, there's no need to despair; feng shui can help you to stabilize these energies or even use them to your advantage. In Sections Two and Three of this book, you'll find plenty of tips that enable you to remove energy leaks and blockages, enliven stagnant chi and protect yourself against harmful energetic vibrations both inside and outside your home.

Retuning the chi

Any changes in colour, objects, light or sounds retune the chi, altering its vibrational qualities. Energy is also generated by the interaction between objects and their surroundings. For example, a house plant may enhance good chi if you put it in your living room, but its energy might be too disruptive for your bedroom.

To achieve the best effect for you, it's vital to create the correct blend of objects and spaces. Be constantly aware of your surroundings – where you work, sleep, rest, eat, make love. In the same way that you think about how you dress, aim to create energy that suits you. The ideal is to produce a balance of strength and flexibility, a state that the feng shui masters called *ou-yeh mo-yeh* – the careful "casting of a sword" – so that its blade and its power are strong and effective.

How can feng shui help you?

Feng shui is not magic, and it can't bring overnight success or rid you of all of life's difficulties. However, it can strengthen periods of good fortune and support you in times of trouble.

Tune a guitar's strings and you stand a better chance of making harmonious, melodic music, but you still need to learn how to play it. Having your car serviced doesn't guarantee you'll never have an accident, but it does mean that when an accident happens, because everything works well, you stand a better chance of survival. So it is with feng shui. The energies that flow around you will affect the way you feel, so service them, tune them and let them flow in harmony with you.

Feeling the force

I can show how feng shui works by explaining how I came to practise it. I was very ill with ME and had to retire early from my job as a headteacher. I tried remedies such as changing my diet and taking vitamin supplements, but nothing helped. Then my doctor suggested meditation and Eastern philosophy to restore my energy levels.

I began to work on my inner self, with meditation, t'ai chi and chi kung, and retuned my environment with feng shui. (In fact, I sometimes describe feng shui as t'ai chi or acupuncture for your surroundings.) Gradually, as I improved the flow of energy within and around me, I got better. I went on to use my skills in all sorts of situations, from balancing the energies in Cardiff's Millennium Stadium, in Wales, to giving private consultations to boost people's health, careers and relationships.

I don't want to suggest, though, that feng shui is a miracle cure. It can help you create an environment in which you can flourish, but if you want to change your life you have to make the decisions and carry them through yourself. In the words of a Buddhist saying, "I can give you the ticket but you've got to catch the train."

The start of your journey

You're about to begin a fascinating journey of discovery. You don't have to believe in the symbolism – just try out the advice. As you work on your home or office, you'll find yourself living in an increasingly harmonious environment, and you'll begin to notice changes for the better in your life. Sometimes, improvements can happen fairly quickly; sometimes they take a longer time, so you need to be patient. Indeed, feng shui can have profound effects on your life, but it is not a "quick fix".

Feng shui is just one piece of the jigsaw puzzle of life, but it's a key piece, which enables you to see the whole picture before you. Simply use it, enjoy it, live it. Feng shui can eventually work for everyone, just as it has worked so well for me.

> "THIS IS THE MOMENT OF EMBARKING.
> ALL AUSPICIOUS SIGNS ARE IN PLACE."
>
> CHINESE PROVERB

HOW TO USE THIS BOOK

Feng shui is a subtle and complex art. A skilled practitioner giving a full consultation will create a blend of energies that is uniquely suited to the client, the energy of their surroundings and the ways in which the client wants to change their life. However, the fundamental ideas and techniques are easy for anyone to learn.

Practical information

To apply feng shui, you need to identify the energies at work in each part of a space. The next few pages show you how to do this, by first drawing a plan of the space, then overlaying the plan with a template called a pa kua (see opposite), which divides a space into nine sectors.

Section One of this book will give you the background information for your work, and will explain the characteristics of different types of energy, including the energies in each sector of the pa kua. Section Two gives guidelines on how to make the most of any room, wherever it's located, and deal with possible problems. Section Three will show you how to respond to the energies surrounding your home, and how to refresh the chi in your home if you're redecorating or selling it.

At the back of the book you'll find a set of practical tools: guides to colours and accessories that you can apply in different areas, followed by a glossary, then a list of websites and books for further information.

Modern solutions

I try to keep things simple and in tune with modern tastes as much as possible. For example, my remedies usually involve items that you may already have, such as pictures, rather than special feng shui items, such as ornaments of Buddha or three-legged toads. I also show how modern technology, such as televisions and computers, can actually benefit you instead of draining your energy.

The pa kua – an essential tool

The chi, or energy, of a space can take various forms. It can be yin or yang (see page 32); it can be ruled by an element, such as metal, earth or water (see page 33); or it can be associated with the main points of the compass, known in feng shui as the Eight Locations (see page 36).

The full pa kua (see page 40; whose name means "eight shapes") shows the qualities, colours and elements associated with each of the Eight Locations. The simplified diagram below shows just the eight

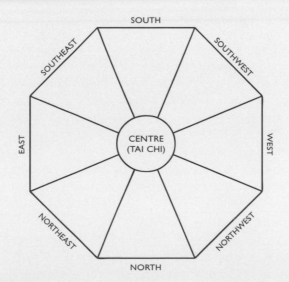

compass locations plus the centre. The pa kua is always used with south at the top and north at the bottom.

It's best to use a full pa kua (see page 40) printed or photocopied onto a transparent acetate sheet, so you can lay it over your floor plan and still see the plan underneath.

Drawing a plan

You'll need paper (squared paper is best), a pencil, a pen and a compass. First, draw a floor plan of the space; see the example opposite. If your house is square or rectangular, simply draw it as it is, preferably to scale. However, if your house is an odd shape, extend the edges of the plan with dotted lines to fill in the "missing" areas and turn it back into a square or rectangle. Then just draw the rooms in proportion to each other; for example, show whether the kitchen is smaller than the hallway and whether the living room is bigger than the dining room.

For each room, mark the position of doors and windows, and show fixed items such as bathtubs, ovens, kitchen cabinets and fireplaces. If your house has two floors, draw a plan for each floor and mark the position of the staircase. Make sure the plan of the upper floor fits exactly over the plan of the lower one, as the floors do in real life.

Finding the centre of the space

The next step is to use a technique called "applying the diagonals" to find the centre of the space. Draw diagonal lines connecting opposite corners. Where the diagonals cross, mark the point with a black spot. This central point (*tai chi*) is called the "earthpot". If you have missing areas, and have used dotted lines to turn them back into squares or rectangles, draw your diagonals from the corners of the "square" or "rectangle", not from the actual edge of the odd-shaped space.

A sample floor plan

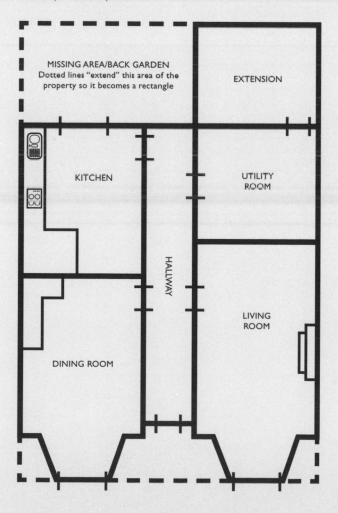

MISSING AREA/BACK GARDEN
Dotted lines "extend" this area of the property so it becomes a rectangle

EXTENSION

KITCHEN

UTILITY ROOM

HALLWAY

LIVING ROOM

DINING ROOM

Taking compass readings

Lay the pa kua template (see page 15) over your floor plan, placing the central section over the black spot marking the centre of your house. Walk to this central point and take a compass reading to find out where north is located.

You'll also need to take extra compass readings at the front door, at the back door and in a few rooms to make sure that you're

 locating north accurately. (If you have a lot of metal objects or electrical equipment close to the compass, these items can interfere with the compass and falsify a reading.) Then line up the north sector of the pa kua with north on your compass.

Applying the pa kua to your plan

Finally, mark all the pa kua sectors, including the centre, onto your plan. If your building has two or more floors, mark the pa kua sectors for every floor. First, do the plan for the lowest floor, then lay your plan for each higher floor on top, so the outlines of the two plans match. Lay both plans on a window pane, so you can use the lower one as a guide, and mark in the pa kua sectors for the upper floor.

Including gardens and grounds

If you have a modest-sized garden or backyard (not several acres), just continue the edges of the pa kua sectors outward from your house, until they cover the whole garden. However, if you have huge grounds, you'll need to apply the diagonals to the whole site plan and then overlay the pa kua. Once again, if the plan is not square or rectangular, you need to fill in the missing areas by drawing dotted lines to make it into a regular shape, in the same way as for a house.

The finished diagram

The pa kua will divide your floor plan into eight "apple pie slices" together with a central area, as shown in the diagram below. You can now see which rooms upstairs and down fall into which pa kua sectors. Some of your rooms may occupy more than one sector (for example, the dining room may spread over the south and the southwest); this is normal. Your diagram will also show which pa kua sectors are cut short by missing parts or enlarged by extensions, if your property is an irregular shape. With the information in your completed diagram, you'll be ready to assess and work on the chi in that space.

Pa kua overlaid on sample floor plan

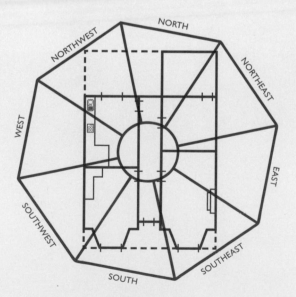

FENG SHUI BASICS

- -

Feng shui is the channelling and blending of chi, the subtle energy that flows through everything in the universe. It is a blend of mystical ideas and practical techniques. Although it originated in China thousands of years ago, its legends and traditions are still relevant to our lives today. This section introduces you to the thoughts and beliefs underlying feng shui, to give you some insight into this ancient art.

古代的才智

HISTORY OF FENG SHUI
Ancient wisdom

Feng shui has grown over many centuries through a blend of practicality and spirituality. It originated in ancient China, where people paid close attention to the natural world. Like many ancient peoples, they explained the features of their world with symbolism and metaphor. This chapter shows how the ancient Chinese blended everyday observation with their spiritual beliefs to create feng shui as we know it today.

The underlying principles

The basic concept in feng shui is that our surroundings contain and give out subtle spiritual energy. In the beginning, the Chinese associated different features in the landscape with particular forms of energy, and they associated these energies with symbolic animals. Later, they used a compass to identify the energies in particular locations. The spiritual beliefs associated with feng shui are rooted in the ancient Chinese philosophy of Taoism (see below), which provided an explanation for the flow of spiritual energy, or chi, through our universe and ourselves.

Origins of feng shui

The awareness of subtle energies in the landscape is thought to have emerged in prehistoric times, from people simply watching nature: observing trees, mountains, water and the weather, and living in harmony with their surroundings. In China, people were particularly aware of the power of wind, or typhoons (*feng*), and water, or floods (*shui*).

The discipline of feng shui originated in hilly northern China 4,000–5,000 years ago. Its first practical application was in positioning grave sites. For a living family to have good luck, it was thought that the graves of their ancestors had to be protected from typhoons or floods. Damaged grave sites, to the ancient Chinese, meant bad luck or bankruptcy for three generations. For this reason, people carefully assessed the landscape for features such as hills, trees and buildings, which would shield sites from the wind. They also took care to avoid locations that were too close to rivers or streams, where flooding or soil erosion could occur. They gradually came to use these skills to protect their crops and houses as well.

The Four Celestial Animals

The prehistoric Chinese associated the cardinal points of the compass (north, south, east and west) with especially powerful energies. They represented these energies symbolically with the Four Celestial Animals: the tortoise, dragon, phoenix and tiger. Images of these animals have been found on pottery dating back over 4,000 years.

In Chinese mythology, the four animals were originally constellations of stars. They fell to earth during a battle in which the Chinese were

TORTOISE	DRAGON	PHOENIX	TIGER
Location: north	Location: east	Location: south	Location: west
Colour: black	Colour: azure/green	Colour: red	Colour: white
Element: water	Element: wood	Element: fire	Element: metal
Symbolizes: protection, progress	Symbolizes: good fortune	Symbolizes: success, completion	Symbolizes: creative energy

fighting each other; the warriors made so much noise that the constellations were dislodged from heaven. The black tortoise fell to the north and became known as the "warrior protector". The red phoenix fell to the south and became the symbol of success and completion. The azure dragon fell to the east and became the symbol of good fortune. The white tiger fell to the west and became the symbol of creativity.

The energy of the north was protective and progressive, and was associated with water (see The Five Elements, page 33). That of the east encouraged growth and ambition, and was associated with wood; it was a highly yang, male energy (see Yin and yang, page 32). South energy was warm, passionate and outgoing, and was associated with fire. The energy of the west, associated with metal, was creative but unpredictable and dangerous, and had to be controlled; it was a very yin, female energy. In feng shui today, people still work with the energies of the Celestial Animals.

Animal energies in the landscape

The Four Celestial Animals are seen as powerful forces in the land-scape surrounding every building. The coiling dragon is said to exist to the east of a site. The sleeping tiger exists in the west, the phoenix is located in the south and the tortoise is found in the north.

According to feng shui, the ideal site for a building should have higher hills behind and to the east of the building, to accommodate the dragon; lower hills in the west, for the tiger, and a small hill in the south, for the phoenix. These principles are still followed today, when people apply feng shui to analyze the locations of houses (see page 124) and arrange the layout of gardens and backyards (see pages 107 and 112).

The dragon and tiger are the most powerful energies. They are believed to be entwined with each other, so a blend of their energies will benefit any site. It is said that wherever the dragon exists, the tiger will also live. For this reason, and because the tiger's energy is so unpredictable and dangerous, feng shui teaches that you shouldn't use any images or symbols of tigers in your house or garden.

The points of the compass

In the beginning, people practised feng shui solely by analyzing the energies of hills and other shapes in the landscape. When the tradition spread to southern China, where the land is flatter with less distinctive features, practitioners of feng shui had to find some other way to assess the flow of energy around them. They started using a compass — originally a metal spoon, magnetized with lodestone, floating in a bowl of water — to detect the energies of different sites. In fact, the compass was used for feng shui centuries before it was used for navigation at sea. Each of the eight main points of the compass therefore came to represent a specific form of energy (see page 36).

The influence of the Tao

Taoism, the philosophy that underlies feng shui, originated in the works of Lao Tzu, who was thought to have lived in the 6th century BC. He wrote a book called The *Tao Te Ching*, which tells of the nature of life in harmony with the universe and brings together many of the concepts of Taoism and feng shui. The Tao is defined as the creative nothingness from which all things are brought into being. From the Tao comes chi, the spiritual energy that exists throughout the universe and in every object.

All things in our universe absorb, contain and give out chi, and all of this chi merges into the Tao: the creative energy behind and within everything. The movement of chi is seen as a continual, swirling flow. Taoists believe the universe to be a vast Oneness, like a tapestry in which every star, creature, rock and drop of water is an essential thread helping to hold all the other threads together. That balance is the basic principle of all existence.

The teachings of Taoism and feng shui were spread by masters – experts who acted as spiritual advisers for their communities. The masters used special techniques, in which common sense and mystical elements were often closely aligned, to enhance the vibrations of chi in people and their surroundings. They blended different energies, using the complementary qualities of yin and yang (see page 32) and the elements of earth, fire, water, metal and wood (see page 33). The practice of tuning the flow of chi in this way still lies at the core of feng shui.

Observing nature

Taoists lived simply, close to nature. Their ideals were to reach a state of creative emptiness (*wu*) and simplicity (*pu*), and to exist in non-action (*wu wei*), a condition that they defined as just being, rather than doing. They believed that enlightenment did not come from deep religious prayer or theory, but rather by the careful observance of nature, landscapes, the weather, the seasons and, in particular, the flowing of water. In this way one could live in harmony, or in resonance, with the chi around and within oneself.

Rolling landscapes with meandering flows of water are one representation of the Tao. The Taoists valued the solitude of the mountains and believed that mountain-tops brought them closer to the sources of chi than anywhere else. They described rolling mountain landscapes as sleeping dragons, rivers as a dragon's veins of flowing blood and the energies of chi as the "dragon's breath" (see also page 39).

The Taoist masters encouraged their communities to take care of the environment. Their prescriptions were often highly practical. For example, they advised people against chopping down large numbers of trees on hillsides, because this could cause mudslides, and told people not to build too close to the bends of rushing, flooding rivers.

Chi on a large scale

As we have seen, hills, trees and other forms in the landscape were all believed to affect the flow of chi. At an agricultural level, chi was the life force that ensured fertile crops, flowers, shrubs and trees. However, the flow of chi could also be detected on a much larger scale.

The energies associated with the points of the compass could, for example, be identified in China itself. The capital, Beijing, was in the north, where the energies support progress in one's career. This was where you were sent if you passed all of your civil service exams (and there were many), to work for the Emperor or the government. The northeast is associated with learning and spirituality, and many Taoist and Buddhist holy places and places of learning were located here.

In the east, where the energies promoted growth, health and good luck, there were fertile lands and wide rivers. The southeast contained the ports, whose richness reflected the abundant energy of this sector. In the south, large ports such as Shanghai connected China to the outside world and embodied the sector's lively, sociable energy. The southwest contained the Gobi Desert and the Himalayas, in which families had to work together and forge strong relationships to survive.

古代的才智

The west and the northwest held the start of the Silk Road, which led westward to the Middle East and enabled new ideas and influences to be brought to China. The Great Wall spread over the north-western northern and northeastern borders protecting China from invaders.

Chi within the body

The masters who practised feng shui also saw the human body as a land. They regarded the environment as the "outer landscape" and the body as the "inner landscape". The two landscapes were related and affected one another; in particular, the larger landscape around people affected the smaller landscape of the body.

Just like an external landscape, the inner landscape of the body has a "dragon" side, which is the left-hand side, and a "tiger" side, which is the right. The head corresponds to the northeast, north and northwest. The northeast governs learning and spirituality; the north is related to protection (like the protection given by the skull) and progress; and the northwest is associated with the removal of obstacles. The centre of the body, 5–8cm (2–3in) below the navel, contains an area called the "furnace" (*tan tien*), where physical energy is believed to be generated. The digestive and urinary systems are like flowing streams and waterfalls, which clear away waste and help the body to work properly.

Channelling the body's energies

Taoists saw the body, like the Tao itself, as a unity. As long as all of the parts cooperated with one another, the body would stay healthy; conflict, however, would destroy it. People could enhance the free flow of chi throughout the body by following practices such as t'ai chi, acupuncture, Chinese medicine and martial arts, particularly kung fu. These disciplines were designed to control or minimize rushing, blocked and disrupted energies in the same way that feng shui did in people's surroundings. As a follower of Taoist teachings, I practise t'ai chi, chi gung and meditation every day. In t'ai chi, you start at the centre of your body and work through all eight locations of the compass, gathering, moving and protecting the body's natural energies.

Feng shui traditions today

The blend of tradition and symbolism that developed in ancient China formed the basis of the four schools of feng shui that exist today: Form School, Compass School, Flying Star and Black Hat. This book is based on what I consider to be the most traditional disciplines: the Taoist Form School, which is focused on the shapes in the landscape, hills, valleys and water; and the Compass School, based on the eight main locations of the compass. I use these methods in my consultations and believe that they will provide you with a wide range of ancient skills for effective and harmonious modern living.

THE REALITY OF THE HOUSE IS ORDER,
THE BLESSING OF THE HOUSE IS CONTENTMENT,
THE GLORY OF THE HOUSE IS HOSPITALITY.
CHINESE TAOIST PROVERB

PRINCIPLES OF FENG SHUI

The dragon's breath

Feng shui encompasses a wide range of remedies, both traditional and modern, for channelling and blending the chi within a space. These treatments can be as simple as using good interior design, such as laying out rooms in a pleasing way and choosing attractive colours, lights, furnishing and accessories. However, I feel that it's best to have some understanding of the theories underlying feng shui so you can apply it with care and full understanding.

In this chapter, I outline the principles with which you'll be working and then give you some tips on how to apply them. This information leads you into Section 2, where I show you, in much more detail, how feng shui works in different rooms and areas.

Three types of luck

In the West, we sometimes say someone is lucky and leave it at that, but in eastern Asia, especially China, they will actually tell you *why* someone is lucky. The Chinese say there are three levels of life: heavenly, earthly and human ("people"). On an ancient Chinese coin, for example, the outer rim symbolizes heaven, the middle represents people and the square hole in the centre symbolizes the earth.

Each level is associated with one form of luck. Heavenly luck is your destiny, or karma (see page 9): the balance of good and bad deeds that you will have inherited from many previous lifetimes. You will either be in credit or be overdrawn, and this state will affect your present lifetime. People luck, sometimes called "merit", has to do with your actions and attitudes. Good thoughts and deeds in this lifetime

LOCARD'S EXCHANGE PRINCIPLE

Every contact leaves a trace. This saying, formulated by the French forensic scientist Edmond Locard, is known as Locard's exchange principle. It means that when you enter a place, you leave something of yourself there and take something away. This idea also occurs in feng shui. Your chi constantly blends with the chi around you, so the energy of your environment will strongly affect you.

can affect your karma from previous lifetimes. (As a Taoist/Buddhist, I am constantly trying to improve my merit, to increase my balance of heavenly luck.) Earthly luck is the combination of energies in your environment, which envelop you and affect you.

Feng shui acts mainly on your earthly luck, so it can affect a third of your total luck. However, it can also make you feel more positive and helpful, and encourage you to be more considerate toward other people and your surroundings; these changes improve your merit as well, which ultimately benefits your heavenly luck.

Tao and chi

The principles of feng shui are based principally on the teachings of Taoism (see page 25). We can draw on the Tao, the source of the chi energy around us, by using the vibrations of appropriate light, colours and objects in a space.

From Tao comes yin and yang (see overleaf), opposites that attract and complement each other. In turn, yin and yang encompass five elements: earth, water, fire, metal and wood (see page 33). These energies are always moving, changing and adjusting their relationships with each other. Everything is built up from yin/yang opposites – negative/positive, dark/light, night/day – trying to become each other or help each other, and form a blend or an "alchemy" (*lien chin shu*) of the five elements. Change is the only constant in the Tao.

Yin and yang

Every object is formed from a blend of yin and yang chi. Yin chi is a more stable, earthy, passive, receptive energy. Yang chi is more strong, positive and transforming. Originally, the word *yin* referred to the dark side of a hill or mountain where the sun did not reach, and *yang* to the light side illuminated by the sun. The meaning of yin and yang eventually widened in much the same way that the application of feng shui, once used only for grave sites, then for crops, extended to be used in houses and gardens. (The concepts of negative and positive energy even occur in modern physics, as in negatively and positively charged particles.)

The yin–yang cycle

The illustration opposite shows the two forms of chi. The dark areas represent yin, and the pale or white areas represent yang. The dots within each area, and the curving boundary between the two, show how the energies are intermingled, so yang contains yin, and vice versa. The circular shape represents the way in which the energies follow a cycle, constantly changing and striving to become each other. As soon as yang reaches its peak, yin is created, and vice versa.

Feng shui is a careful blending of yin and yang. Total yin or total yang is not healthy; we need a combination of both to achieve harmony. Nature does a superb job of balancing the two energies, but human environments and activities constantly disrupt this equilibrium. A house can favour more active yang energy, or it can be oriented toward slower yin energy, and each room has its own energetic balance. By deciding what you wish to achieve from your surroundings, you can get the yin/yang balance just right (see page 134).

YANG QUALITIES
Strong
Light
Positive
Transforming

YIN QUALITIES
Stable
Dark
Passive
Receptive

The Five Elements

From the Tao, the underlying energy of the universe, come yin and yang, opposite forms of energy that attract and complement each other. From yin and yang, in turn, arise the forms known as the Five Elements: earth, water, fire, metal and wood.

These elements are different from the four elements of air, fire, earth and water that are familiar in Western culture; they are defined as "forces" or "movers", rather than actual substances. They are seen as moving swirls of chi, which are constantly changing. In Chinese, the Five Elements are called *wu hsing*, "the five things that are being done". They don't so much cause good or bad things to happen as create a pattern in which certain things are likely to happen.

The elements are associated with the points of the compass (see page 23) and are shown on the pa kua, the design template used to define sectors of a space in feng shui (see page 140). Wood represents east (and southeast); fire, south; metal, west (and northwest); and water, north. Earth, or equilibrium, is the natural balance of the other four elements, appearing in the centre of the pa kua (as well as in the north-east and southwest pa kua sectors).

In feng shui, symbolic objects and colours are used to stimulate the energy of the elements. The most obvious symbols are fire and water, stones (earth), and wooden or metal objects. Each element is also associated with certain colours; for example, reds symbolize fire, yellows and browns represent earth, and white and grey symbolize metal.

The cycles of chi

Each element is associated with a specific form of chi. Wood represents the rising chi of morning, spring and growing things. Fire represents mid-day and summer: the state of maximum vitality. Metal, linked to sunset and autumn, is a declining state of changing patterns. Water, associated with night and winter, is a state of rest. They follow the cycle of yin and yang; fire is the most yang form and metal and water are the most yin.

Chi can move from one element to another in two ways, known as the Constructive Cycle and the Destructive Cycle. The two cycles are shown opposite. In the Constructive Cycle, the chi follows a curving, circular path. Each element gives helpful energy to the ones on either side; so, for example, water supports wood and metal, and wood supports water and fire. In the Destructive Cycle, however, the circle is interrupted. Chi from each element moves in straight lines, bypassing the next element and controlling the following one; so, for example, fire destroys (melts) metal, and metal destroys (chops down) wood.

Making use of the cycles

Both cycles are important for creating good feng shui. Helpful elements
in the Constructive Cycle can stimulate beneficial chi in a pa kua sector.
For example, water features can enhance the energy of the southeast
pa kua sector, which is governed by wood.

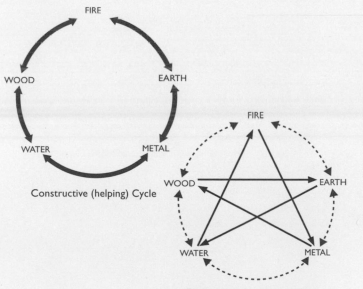

Constructive (helping) Cycle

Destructive (controlling) Cycle

On the other hand, the elements in the Destructive Cycle can block
each other, so you can actually use them to create a protective barrier
to harmful energies. The Destructive Cycle is particularly useful in
bathrooms, where you add earth symbols to the decor so you can
control the overpowering water energy.

龍
气

The Eight Locations

Each cardinal point of the compass – north, south, east and west – is associated with a specific form of chi (see page 23). The other main points (northeast, northwest, southeast and southwest) are also linked with particular energies. Not only does the chi differ in each compass position, but each form of chi also represents different aspects of your life. These points form the Eight Locations recognized in feng shui.

TRIGRAMS AND MAGIC SQUARE NUMBERS

- **NORTH (1)** governs career and progress. The chi is calm and restful, but also strong, stable and protective.
- **NORTHEAST (8)** relates to spirituality, knowledge and learning. The chi is sharp and changeable.
- **EAST (3)** governs health, family, ambition and longevity. The chi is nurturing and promotes growth.
- **SOUTHEAST (4)** represents "richness of life". The chi in this sector brings great opportunities.
- **SOUTH (9)** symbolizes fame, sociability and communication. The chi in this sector is fiery and passionate.
- **SOUTHWEST (2)** is the sector associated with couples, romance and physical relationships. The chi is calm and solid.
- **WEST (7)** represents children, pleasure, creativity and new projects. Its energy is lively, unpredictable and can be dangerous.
- **NORTHWEST (6)** is associated with mentors or other helpful people, important meetings and the removal of obstacles. The chi in this sector is strong and reassuring; the Chinese say it's "like a kindly father" (jen t'zu).

The points are referred to as "locations" rather than "directions" because they refer to sectors of a space (like slices of an apple pie) in which colours or objects are placed, rather than directions that these items face. The Eight Locations are shown on the pa kua (see page 140). Each is associated with a particular element and group of colours, and with a number on the "magic square" (see below). In addition, each is represented by a trigram (see opposite), which is a symbol showing the blend of yin and yang energies. Each trigram is made up of three lines: broken lines (yin), solid lines (yang) or a combination of the two.

The locations in your home

When you apply the pa kua to your home or other spaces (see page 18), you simply need to define which locations are occupied by each room. Bear in mind that the boundaries between locations are only approximate; each location blends into the next, so you can't accurately stand with one foot in the north and one foot in the northeast.

In the pa kua, the central point (*tai chi*), or "earthpot", is a place of very special energy flow, with yin and yang energies swirling around it. When you're working on an area, you should always try to leave the *tai chi* as clear space, making sure it never becomes blocked.

The magic square (*lo shu*)

The *lo shu*, or magic square, is another traditional tool in feng shui. It is a square divided into nine smaller squares, each of which contains a number from 1 to 9. If you add the numbers horizontally, vertically or diagonally, they always total 15.

The *lo shu* is said to have been discovered when a Taoist sage saw a turtle creep out of a river, and noticed a particular pattern of cracks on the turtle's shell. (In ancient China, one method of fortune-telling was to look at the cracks on the backs of tortoises or turtles.) The sage observed that each square of the turtle's shell had a different number of marks, ranging from 1 to 9.

The magic square and the pa kua

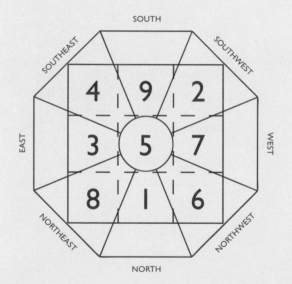

The symbolism of the numbers

The numbers contained in the magic square came to be included in the pa kua, and each is associated with a particular location. For example, 1 represents the north and symbolizes the beginning of all things, and 9 represents the south and symbolizes completion and success. Other examples include 2, which represents the southwest and symbolizes loving couples, and 7, which represents the creativity of the west. The most auspicious numbers are 1 and 9; the latter is extremely lucky because it is formed from 8, symbolizing earth, and 1, symbolizing heaven – the perfect mix or "alchemy". The most powerful number is 5, which represents the centre, or *tai chi*.

The *lo shu* is also associated with the cycle of yin and yang energy. Even numbers hold yin energy, and odd numbers have yang energy. In ancient Chinese belief, 15 (the sum of the numbers in each row, column and diagonal line of the square) is the halfway point of the lunar cycle, or the number of days it takes the moon to go from new to full. It represents the transition from waxing to waning, when the energy begins to go from yang to yin.

Good and bad chi: the dragon's breath

The ancient Chinese referred to the perfect combination of yin and yang chi as the "dragon's breath" (*sheng chi*). They described healthy chi as constantly flowing (*liu tung*) or changing and moving (*tung te*). Feng shui practitioners were known as "dragon-masters", whose job was to "light the eye of the dragon" – in other words, to work on the chi in and around a building to bring it to life and stimulate a beneficial flow.

When feng shui was first developed (see page 22), people identified the dragon's breath with protective mountains and  hills that produced wood, fruits and water. If the energy was too yang and forceful, it would attack people's homes, crops and grave sites. If the dragon's breath was too yin and sluggish, it was thought to bring on disease and bad crops. (In fact, harmful chi can be seen as either too "feng", like a fierce wind, or too "shui", like stagnant water.)

龍气

Stimulating the dragon's breath

The concept of the dragon's breath is still important in feng shui today. Ideally, chi should move in a measured and meandering way, flowing in a curved path around a space, neither stagnant nor rushing. These gentle flows are a source of clear-headedness, health and contentment.

Chi that rushes in straight lines will be too yang and will produce stress, frustration and anger. One particularly harmful form of yang chi comes from "poison arrows" — sharp corners within or outside your house, that direct negative energy at you. On the other hand, still, stagnant chi, as found in dark alcoves, can make you depressed and lethargic. You therefore need to organize spaces and choose furnishings that help the chi to flow constantly, in gentle, curving patterns.

Achieving moderation

Use feng shui remedies in moderation so that they are appropriate for you and your surroundings. Take care not to go too far, otherwise you will end up with the opposite of what you are searching for.

Some people using feng shui fall into this trap: they think that the larger the ornaments and the brighter the colours they use, the better the result will be. This is not true. As the Chinese say, "Overdo the medicine and it becomes poison". For example, water and symbols of water, such as mirrors and the colour blue, can be energizing, but if you use too many of these symbols in a space, they produce excessively powerful energy and therefore become enemies, not friends.

The ABC of feng shui

Awareness, Balance and Control constitute the ABC of feng shui. Following these three principles will help you achieve a perfect blend of energies. First, you need to be *aware* of the space around you. Look at

APPLYING FENG SHUI: THE ABC

Awareness of the energies (*chih chueh te*) is the first step in applying feng shui. The Chinese use the expression "awareness is a weapon" (*chih hai te wu ch'i*). Carefully observe the flows of energy through a building or garden.

 Next comes **Balance** (*ping heng*). To achieve the correct balance for your personality and needs, you need to balance yin and yang, and blend different elements, to make the energy flow at the speed you want.

Control (*kuan li*), or calmness (*chen ching te*), is the ideal result. Once you have applied feng shui correctly, you will have a harmonious environment that will support you as you improve your health, feelings and life.

the positions of doors, windows, edges and corners, and find any nooks and crannies. *Balance* the flow of the chi by applying feng shui, then you can *control* and use the energies effectively.

The correct mix of energies will support, encourage and protect you as you face the demands of everyday life. However, any imbalance may reveal itself in your life as problems, stress or even illness.

Applying feng shui in the modern world

Using feng shui today means finding solutions that fit in with modern life. On the one hand, 21st-century life offers conveniences such as electric lighting, gas fires, myriad colours in paints and furnishing and central heating. On the other hand, though, the natural environment is disrupted and polluted by factors such as electrical appliances in the home or busy roads outside. It's important, therefore, to be able to control the chi coming from outside your home. Feng shui is a way of "restoring the celestial amidst the mundane", bringing back positive chi. (For specific examples of the challenges in today's environment, and feng shui solutions to them, see Chapter 12.)

Working with what you have

The practice of feng shui can be as simple or as complex as you like – but let common sense be your guide. Although feng shui has its mystical elements, it need not lead to weird and wonderful remedies, or radical changes to your house. If I'm working with an architect on building a house, then we can make sure the structure has good feng shui from the start. However, if you're working on an existing property, you don't need the sort of extreme measures that give the art a bad name, such as knocking down walls or moving the front door.

Traditional feng shui can involve the use of objects such as Buddhas, three-legged toads, crystals and wind chimes. If you like these ornaments, feel free to use them, but you don't have to if they're not to your taste. You need to work on the general energies of a space, rather than fix on specific objects to provide you with luck, love or prosperity. I really enjoy working on places where the natural energy feels fantastic but there are no clues of feng shui around – just really good colour and design.

You simply need to work with things as they are. The aim is to bring your life into harmony and balance with your surroundings. This book will show you how, by advising you how to blend yin and yang, the Five Elements and the Eight Locations.

Making changes happen

Before you begin work, you need to set your intentions for your whole property (see page 134). Next, you need to find out which areas of the property fall into which sectors of the pa kua (see pages 18–19), so you can find out where the most favourable flows of chi are located. Then you need to work out how to produce new chi or enhance existing chi, by using the information in Sections Two and Three. Using feng shui will help you to make sure that the energy is in harmony (ho sheng) and working with you.

Solving problems

Feng shui solutions involve either enhancing beneficial chi or controlling harmful chi. You can boost good chi by rearranging objects in a space and clearing clutter; by adding light, using mirrors, spotlights or uplighters; or by using colours and plants that suit the pa kua sector, or that symbolize a "friendly" element (see the Constructive Cycle of the elements, page 35). These remedies help the chi to flow in a gentle, curving path. To protect yourself from harmful chi, you can block the energy by using the Destructive Cycle of the elements (see page 35), hide the source in a closet or behind a screen or door, or, if possible, remove the problem altogether.

Putting it all into practice

The next section will show you how to put these ideas into practice. Each chapter deals with a particular room or space. I explain how chi should ideally move in that area, and give examples of good and bad chi in action. There is also special advice, called "doctor's orders", for certain problems. The chapters end with suggestions on enhancing the chi for that specific room, depending on which pa kua sector it occupies.

ROOM BY ROOM

This section shows you how to enhance the chi in your home, garden and work space. It doesn't matter if your home is not perfect according to feng shui principles; you can improve any space. Here, you'll find practical suggestions designed to suit your everyday life and your natural tastes in interior design, as well as some innovative solutions for creating just the right blend of energies for you.

入
口

FRONT DOOR, HALLWAY AND STAIRS
Mouth

Chi filters into a house through the walls, doors, windows and roof. A lot of it comes through the front door, which, in feng shui, is called the "mouth" (*kou*). You need to let good chi in through the *kou* but keep bad chi out – a process called "feeding the mouth, energizing the home".

Once inside your home, chi flows along hallways, through the rooms and up and down staircases. You need to keep these areas uncluttered and well used so the chi can circulate freely and benefit your home.

Feeding your front door

The front door, or *kou*, connects your home to the outside world. Just as you need your mouth for eating, drinking and breathing, the *kou* is vital because it lets the chi into your home – so you have to "feed it" well.

WU FU LIN MEN

The Chinese have a saying, "May the five blessings approach the door" (*wu fu lin men*) – the blessings being health, wealth, longevity, an auspicious life and a natural death.

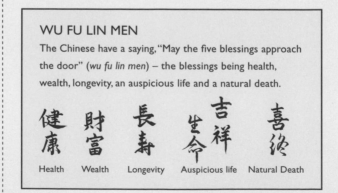

| Health | Wealth | Longevity | Auspicious life | Natural Death |

A protective front door

SMALL PANES OF GLASS

OUTSIDE LIGHTS

METAL NUMBERS

METAL DOOR KNOCKER

METAL DOOR KNOB

METAL MAILBOX

STEPS UP TO DOOR

PLANT POTS

The suggestions given here are for a house, but will also help to nourish your front door if you live in an apartment.

Bright lights just inside and outside the door are an excellent way to attract good chi. You need a constant light, not security lights that only come on for a few minutes at a time; it's best to leave them on all night, or at least from dusk until bedtime.

Ideally, your front door should be solid, or have only small glass panes. A door with a lot of glass will let energy leak out of the *kou* – it's like having your mouth open all the time. You can stop this energy loss by fitting a roller blind over the glass or having a curtain behind the door.

Deflecting harmful chi

Check outside the door for "poison arrows" that can aim harmful chi at your home (see pages 126–7). To deflect this chi, use shiny metal fixtures, such as door knockers (see previous page). Alternatively, put rounded plant pots on either side of the front door, with suitable plants for the pa kua sector (see page 146). If you have a porch with pillars, it will shield the door, and if you have steps up to your door you're especially lucky: traditional legends say that demons can't climb steps!

For further protection, you could put an ornament or a photograph of a dog in the hall, facing the door, because dogs give out protective energy. Or, if you have a dog, put his or her bed near the door.

The threshold

On the left-hand side of the threshold, as you face the front door from inside, put up a "flowing, good water" symbol to boost the flow of chi. You could have a small picture of a waterfall, a shell, a model boat or even an abstract blue painting. Or put up a rounded mirror with a frame that suits the pa kua sector. Hang it at the height of the tallest person in your home so it won't "chop off" the top of their head.

Make sure your water symbol or mirror doesn't reflect the front door, or else you'll push away a lot of good chi entering the *kou*. Never place a mirror or lucky ornament opposite a kitchen or bathroom door because it will increase bad energy (*pei pu shan te*) from those areas.

Enhancing your hallway

Chi needs to curve and meander along a hallway, not rush through or become blocked. The best hallways are fairly wide, letting chi flow gently along them and through the house. However, even if your hallway isn't ideal, you can use lighting and other measures to improve it.

Calming the chi in a hallway

A long, narrow hallway forces chi to rush through it, like a strong river in a gorge. The problem will be worse if there are three doors in line, including the front and back doors. To steady the flow, place mirrors in a staggered pattern along the hallway so the chi will curve from one to the next. Hang the first mirror as the "flowing, good water" symbol on the left-hand side of the front door (see Threshold, opposite). Hang the next one further down, on the right, and so on.

If your hallway has sharp bends in it, mirrors can also counteract "poison arrows" of harmful energy coming from the corners. Hang the mirrors as shown in the diagram below, so they'll encourage the chi to flow smoothly around the corners.

Smoothing out corners in a hallway

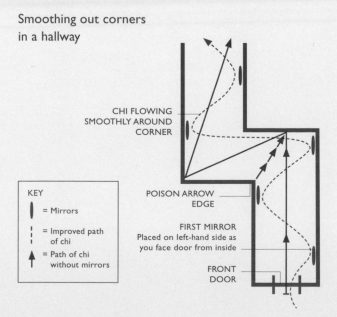

CHI FLOWING SMOOTHLY AROUND CORNER

POISON ARROW EDGE

KEY

❙ = Mirrors

⋮ = Improved path of chi

↑ = Path of chi without mirrors

FIRST MIRROR
Placed on left-hand side as you face door from inside

FRONT DOOR

入口

DOCTOR'S ORDERS

Problem: You have a long, narrow hallway, but you don't want to fill it with mirrors.

Remedy: If mirrors don't suit your taste, you can regulate the flow of chi by laying floorboards running across the hallway. An easier solution is simply to put down rounded, non-slip rugs, in colours appropriate to the pa kua location (see pages 143–5), at intervals along the hallway.

Working with wide hallways

If your hallway is a huge, wide, echoing space, chi may flow too sluggishly through it. To help the chi move faster, lift the energy with richer, more vivid colours and lots of bright lighting. Floorboards pointing lengthwise along the wide hallway can also stimulate a more vigorous flow of chi.

The benefits of plants

Large, broad-leaved plants, such as rubber plants or Swiss cheese plants, can be ideal in a hallway, as long as they suit the pa kua sector (see page 53). If you have two doors in a line, put a plant beside one of them so it steadies the flow of chi from that door to the next one. Plants can also enhance chi, especially in dark alcoves and against corners of walls.

Balancing the energies in a hallway

The ideal blend of chi in a hallway should be slightly balanced toward yang, to promote strength, protection and activity in your home. To stimulate yang chi, use lots of natural light, good lighting and bright or neutral colours rather than pastels.

If your hallway is dark, then the chi will be too yin and sluggish. To lift the chi, add slightly stronger colours in the form of small accessories; in this way you can enhance the effect without overdoing it.

The decor also needs to include "friendly elements" (*yu shan te yao su*), which support the element of the hallway's pa kua sector (see Constructive Cycle, page 34). For example, in the north sector, which is ruled by water, wooden floors and plants can be beneficial.

Stabilizing scattered chi

In general, choose items with vertical lines, such as banisters, tall plants and vertical blinds; verticals symbolize healthy upward growth. Avoid horizontal lines, as in dado rails (or chair rails) and bookshelves, because they splinter the chi, causing energy to be dispersed. If you have a dado rail, paint the wall and the rail in one colour to stabilize the chi. Highly patterned wallpaper or carpets also disrupt chi. If you have "busy" wallpaper, hanging a clock on the wall will help to remedy this problem. Clocks are ideal in hallways because they stimulate as well as stabilize chi.

Keeping your hallway clear

Try to keep your hallway free of furniture and clutter. If possible, tidy outdoor clothes and cleaning items away — for example, in a closet under the stairs. If the closet contains a fuse box or an electricity meter, place an amethyst crystal on top of the box to help cleanse the negative energy produced by static electricity.

Keep all of the doors off the hallway closed whenever possible — particularly those leading to toilets, bathrooms or kitchens. In fact, it's good to get into the habit of keeping all doors closed, to preserve and build up the chi in each room.

入口

Conserving chi on staircases

Stairs can be a challenge in feng shui terms because chi flows down them like water. Open-riser and spiral staircases are particularly bad; in fact, spiral staircases are traditionally described as a "dagger" (*pi shou*) piercing a building. However, you can easily reduce the loss of chi.

At the bottom of the stairs, you could place a round or oval rug, in a rich colour. If the pa kua location is suitable (see opposite), you could put a broad-leaved plant under or beside the stairs. For an open or spiral staircase, shine an uplighter or lamp upward through the stairs, or put green trailing plants on the outer edge of alternate stairs.

Never put desks, chairs or telephones under stairs, because stairs "squash" the chi beneath them, which can depress your own chi. If the

Reducing the flow of chi down stairs

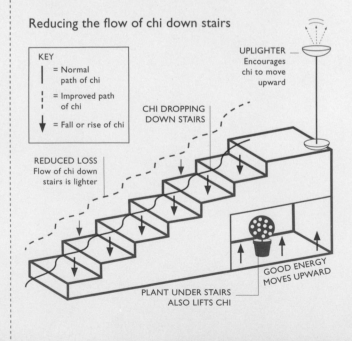

KEY

| = Normal path of chi

⦙ = Improved path of chi

↓ = Fall or rise of chi

UPLIGHTER
Encourages chi to move upward

CHI DROPPING DOWN STAIRS

REDUCED LOSS
Flow of chi down stairs is lighter

GOOD ENERGY MOVES UPWARD

PLANT UNDER STAIRS ALSO LIFTS CHI

space is open, put a light or a large plant there to lift the chi; otherwise, use it as a closet for storage (see page 51).

Stairs facing the front door can let chi escape out of the house. You can stop this energy loss by installing spotlights, with one pointing just above the front door and one at the stairs, to "move them apart".

An uplifting picture facing the top of the stairs can attract helpful chi. Suitable subjects depend on the pa kua sector; for example, an abstract or humorous picture in the west can enhance creative energies.

Location, location, location

North: A north hallway can make you feel rather isolated, but you can remedy this problem by boosting the chi in the south of the house. Wood symbols, such as wooden floors and plants, are beneficial in the north.

Northeast: The chi in a northeastern hall can cause frustration, but you can counteract the problem with earthy colours and strong lighting. Crystal, and shiny metal ornaments and vases, also enhance the chi.

East, southeast, south: These sectors are perfect for front doors and hallways; the chi promotes growth, ambition and success. You can boost the energy with wooden floors and with a few broad-leaved plants.

Southwest: A southwestern hallway gives your house the feel of a sanctuary, but the energy is a bit sluggish. If you need to energize it, use fiery colours, strong lighting and crystal or shiny metal ornaments.

West, northwest: A hallway in the west usually promotes creativity. The chi in the northwest helps with determination, parental authority and removal of obstacles. Metal ornaments can enhance the energy.

LIVING ROOM
Living energy

The chi in a living room needs to be balanced toward lively yang energy, to support pleasure and social activities. Make sure that you have good chi coming into the room, then let it circulate freely. Strong shapes, plants, clocks and ornaments can all help to enhance the chi and make your living room, in feng shui terms, "a place of brightness".

Laying out your living room

Living rooms need to be light and bright. Allow as much natural light as possible into the room. Lights and lamps around the room, especially uplighters, will move the chi upward, turning it from yin to yang. However, avoid having large ceiling-mounted lights directly above people's heads, if possible; they make the yang energy too dominant and harsh.

To keep the chi flowing freely, position your furniture around the edges of the room. Leave the centre (*tai chi*), or "earthpot", clear, except perhaps for a low coffee table, placed so that it isn't blocking the dead centre of the room. Place chairs and sofas against solid walls to make their occupants feel secure. In feng shui, seats shouldn't have their backs to doors or windows, because they leave the occupants in a vulnerable position. Make sure there's plenty of space around the furniture, because overcrowding can block the flow of chi.

Improving problem areas

To create the ideal flow of chi around your living room, you need to find and fix any problem areas. One common source of harmful chi comes from "poison arrows", created by sharp edges or corners pointing

A well planned living room

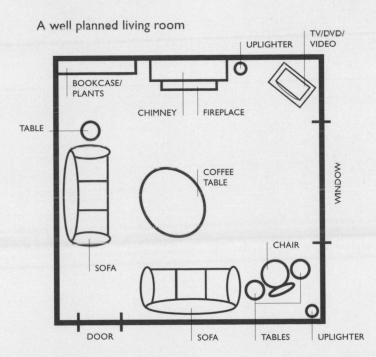

BOOKCASE/
PLANTS

UPLIGHTER

TV/DVD/
VIDEO

CHIMNEY   FIREPLACE

TABLE

COFFEE
TABLE

WINDOW

CHAIR

SOFA

DOOR   SOFA   TABLES   UPLIGHTER

at seated people. Poison arrows give off rushing energy that can make people feel tense. You can neutralize edges and corners by covering them with trailing plants. The horizontal lines of bookshelves, called "strangle lines" (chiao ssu), can also disrupt chi. Glass-fronted bookshelves will prevent this problem; otherwise, just move books forward so they overhang the edges of the shelves, to interrupt the strangle lines.

Alcoves, such as the spaces around a fireplace, can collect pools of stagnant chi, but their edges form poison arrows. Try to avoid having seats in alcoves because the chi can make people feel lethargic. To get the chi moving and to break up poison arrows, place broad-leaved plants in the alcove, if the pa kua sector allows (see page 61), with some of their branches extending beyond the edge, and hang mirrors on protruding walls. Other possible solutions, if they suit the pa kua sector, are uplighters, water features, lava lamps, TVs and music systems.

Protecting windows

Check the windows for poison arrows outside your home (see pages 126–7), such as the corners of buildings, which could direct harmful chi into your living room. To deflect the energy from a poison arrow, hang vertical blinds. Alternatively, you can place protective objects on the window sill, facing the poison arrow. Dogs are a great source of protection, so if you have a dog you could put his or her picture in the window. Clear quartz crystals are also an especially good remedy, but if you prefer you could use a crystal bowl or decanter.

Balancing colours

Generally, strong colours balanced by more neutral ones are ideal in a living room. Bold splashes of colour in cushions, rugs, curtains and pictures work very well, giving the room life. The more vivid the colours, the more rapidly the chi will move. Mid-toned, bright colours produce more yang energy; very pale or dark colours give off yin energy.

If a colour is wrong for a sector, or the right colour doesn't suit your decor, you don't have to redecorate. Just put a piece of furniture, rug, cushion or plant in the correct feng shui colour on top of the wrong one. In feng shui, this is called "placing the bandage". The energy from the item on top overcomes the energy of the underlying colour.

Beams

Wooden beams symbolize chi pressing downward and depress the energy of anything (or anyone) beneath them. Try not to have seats right under a beam. If you can't avoid this problem, you can take various steps to make the beams feel "lighter" and less oppressive.

If the beams are small and you don't mind disguising them, you can paint them the same colour as the ceiling to make them blend in. Otherwise, you can lift the energy by using a picture or other object that symbolizes upward movement.

A traditional remedy is to attach open fans or bamboo flutes to beams, but this can look really out of place in modern homes. Instead, you could use pictures of birds in flight or of hot-air balloons rising. Large plants under beams work very well, as do uplighters or spotlights pointing up at the beam. I remember using the wooden propeller from a vintage aeroplane along a beam in one house. It looked magnificent!

Fireplaces

Every good living room needs a focal point. A working fireplace, whether it uses wood, coal, gas or electricity, can form a wonderful centre. The fire can give the room a very welcoming feel. In addition, it raises, warms and moves the energy.

Ideal pa kua locations for fireplaces are east, southeast, south, southwest and northeast. To boost the fire energy even more in these sectors, hang a picture of poppies or sunflowers, or one with colours symbolizing fire, above the mantelpiece. When you're not using the fireplace, you could place plants, flowers or screens in front of the hearth. A mirror, on the other hand, is a bad choice in these areas because it represents water and "puts the fire out" (hsi mieh).

The west, northwest and north are inauspicious sectors for fireplaces because fire clashes with the ruling elements (metal in the west and northwest, and water in the north). However, you can overcome the problem by using the Destructive Cycle of elements (see page 34) – hanging a large mirror over the fireplace to "put out the fire" is actually a good idea in these sectors. Blend water and metal chi by choosing one with an ornate metal frame (or wood painted silver or gold). A plasma screen TV could go here; when switched off, it acts as a mirror.

In the west or northwest, rounded ornaments in shiny chrome, stainless steel, brass or copper also work well to "put out the fire".

Fireplace in a supportive pa kua sector

PICTURE OF
BRIGHT FLOWERS
supports fire energy

Fireplace in a challenging pa kua sector

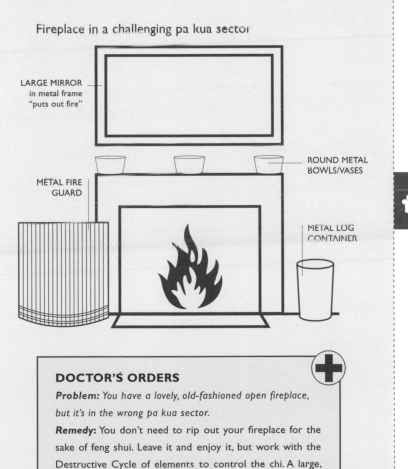

LARGE MIRROR
in metal frame
"puts out fire"

**ROUND METAL
BOWLS/VASES**

**METAL FIRE
GUARD**

**METAL LOG
CONTAINER**

DOCTOR'S ORDERS

Problem: *You have a lovely, old-fashioned open fireplace,
but it's in the wrong pa kua sector.*

Remedy: You don't need to rip out your fireplace for the
sake of feng shui. Leave it and enjoy it, but work with the
Destructive Cycle of elements to control the chi. A large,
ornate mirror, and metal ornaments around the fireplace, all
fit in very well and help to balance the energy.

In the north, use trailing plants such as ivy, which symbolize falling water. Place them on the mantelpiece at either side of the fire, or even have one in front of the fireplace when the fire is out.

Sound and energy

The vibration from sounds, such as music or voices, is an excellent way to boost chi. Feng shui teaches that everything is formed from vibrations (see page 127) and if you create the right vibrations around you, they will support and strengthen your own energy.

A TV, radio or music system can create highly beneficial chi. Electrical items, such as TVs, radios and battery-powered clocks, will energize yang chi in any location. They're useful to boost the energy in alcoves, or in bay windows to shield you from poison arrows. If you have Venetian blinds, a TV or radio in front of them will help to diffuse harmful chi from the horizontal lines. If you play a musical instrument, that can be another good source of sound.

Ornaments and pictures

The most important thing to remember is to surround yourself with decorations that you like. Most people have a mixture of items that they've inherited and pieces that they've chosen themselves. If you like them, keep them, but if they were given to you and aren't to your taste, pass them on or give them to charity. Antiques hold energy from their previous owners and history, so, in order to benefit from them fully, try to find out as much as possible about their history.

Ideally, pictures should be lively, uplifting and attractive. Try to avoid hunting scenes, lonely, windswept landscapes with single figures, or images with sad associations. For best results, match the subject and main colours to the pa kua sector (see opposite, and pages 143–5).

Beneficial plants

Broad-leaved plants, such as rubber plants and Swiss cheese plants, are best for stimulating chi. If you don't want to keep real plants, artificial plastic or silk ones are just as good. Pot pourri is helpful because of the smell. However, avoid dried flowers or ornamental twigs in jars because they hold stagnant energy.

Location, location, location

North: Enhance the chi in a northern living room with wood symbols, such as greens and plants, or metal symbols: whites, creams, chrome and stainless steel. To boost your career, try water or symbols of water.

Northeast: The chi here is ideal for recharging your energy. Focus on earth symbols, such as terracotta, apricot or yellow, granite or marble and unglazed pottery. Crystal is also beneficial. Add touches of metal (see North, above). Electrical items can promote knowledge and learning.

East, southeast, south: The chi in eastern and southeastern living rooms will promote growth and "richness of life"; the south enhances sociability. Use lots of wood symbols, such as the colour green, plants and pictures of countryside or flowers, with yellows and touches of reds. Water symbols in the southeast can help to increase your prosperity.

Southwest: This sector has relaxing energy that nurtures relationships. Blend earth with some metal, as for the northeast (see above).

West, northwest: Living rooms in these sectors can boost energy, determination and creative thinking. The ideal blend of chi is metal, such as whites, creams, and stainless steel, with some earth symbols.

DINING ROOM
Easy digesting

In ancient China, the dining room was seen as the heart of the house (*hsin tsang*). It was believed to be a centre of wealth: not just in terms of money, but also in "richness of life" (*sheng ming ts'ai fu*), quality of living and strong, deeply based relationships.

A comfortable space

The room needs to hold warm, quite slow-moving energy, to encourage "easy digesting" (*hsiao hua jung i te*). It should suggest fine food, pleasure and relaxation. Ideally, eat all your main meals in a dining room or area and spend lots of time there, so you benefit from the energy.

Dining rooms that are fairly wide, and are rectangular or square, have the best feng shui – but you can make the most of any space. As in the living room, you need to work on alcoves in order to help the chi circulate more freely around them (see page 55).

Laying out your dining room

In feng shui, it's best to have a dining room that is separate from your living room and kitchen, and the chi of each room should feel different. However, if you don't have a dining room, an effective solution is to mark out a separate dining area within your kitchen or living room.

One way is to use a piece of furniture, such as a sideboard, sofa or folding screen. If you prefer an open-plan look, you can mark the division by using uplighters, large, broad-leaved evergreen plants or rectangular rugs that suit the pa kua sector. In ancient feng shui, room dividers like these were called "fortress walls" (*yao sai ch'iang pi*).

Dining area created in a kitchen

DOOR

DINING
ROOM
TABLE

WINDOW

KITCHEN

KITCHEN CABINETS
Used to separate kitchen
from dining area

Dining area created in a living room

TV

DOOR

SIDEBOARD

DINING
ROOM
TABLE

WINDOW

LAMP

SEATING
Used to separate living
room from dining area

PLANT

Good and bad positions for a dining table

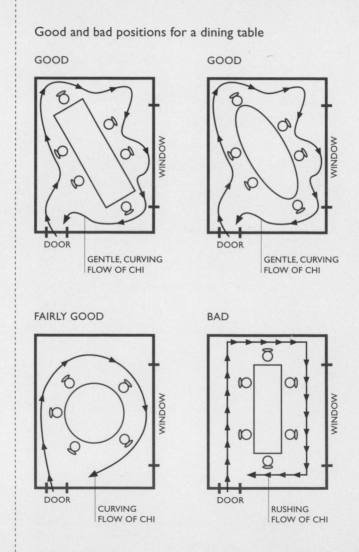

GOOD

GOOD

WINDOW

WINDOW

DOOR

DOOR

GENTLE, CURVING
FLOW OF CHI

GENTLE, CURVING
FLOW OF CHI

FAIRLY GOOD

BAD

WINDOW

WINDOW

DOOR

DOOR

CURVING
FLOW OF CHI

RUSHING
FLOW OF CHI

Choosing and positioning the table

Your dining table should be large but fit comfortably in the room. Oval or round shapes are best, but if your table is rectangular, you can balance it with rounded shapes such as rugs in the rest of the room.

It's best to place the table at the centre of the dining room and turn it at a slight angle in relation to the walls, so the chi will flow in a gentle, curving path around the room. If you put the table straight and parallel with the walls, the chi will be channelled in a straight line through the room or around the edges, and may get trapped in the corners.

Alternatively, you could position the table off-centre, toward one end or corner of the room (see below). If the dining room has two doors facing each other, chi will rush from one door to the other; positioning the table off-centre or at an angle can keep the people seated there out of the way of the fast-flowing energy.

Table and seating positions

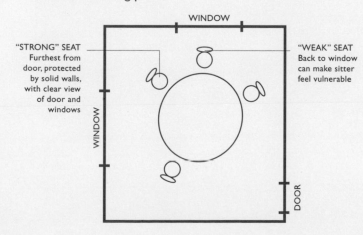

WINDOW

"STRONG" SEAT
Furthest from
door, protected
by solid walls,
with clear view
of door and
windows

WINDOW

"WEAK" SEAT
Back to window
can make sitter
feel vulnerable

DOOR

Seating arrangements

In feng shui, it's good practice to seat the oldest family member or an important guest in the "honoured guest" position at the table. This is the seat furthest from the door, with solid walls behind it and offering a good view of the door and windows. If possible, place all the seats so that no one has his or her back to a door or large window, because this "weak" position may leave that person feeling insecure. This problem is especially likely with round tables, so take particular care with seating.

DOCTOR'S ORDERS

Problem: *You want your family to eat together at the dining table, but arguments keep erupting.*

Remedy: Quieten the energy at the table with soft lighting and pastel colours. Make sure no one is in a "weak" seat (see above), which could make them insecure and defensive. However, if someone is argumentative, you could try seating them in the "weak" position to make them less dominant.

Setting your table

In general, plain colours and simple shapes are best to promote the calming energy you need around the table. If you prefer a pattern, opt for one based on just one or two main colours. Vertical stripes are ideal because they symbolize uplifting energy. However, busy patterns splinter the chi. To get the most benefit from your tableware, keep items in good condition and discard any chipped plates, bowls or glasses.

Boost the energy of your dining table by choosing place mats, napkins, tablecloths and candles in colours or materials that suit the pa kua

Table displays

A rounded bowl filled with rounded fruit, in the centre of the table, is excellent feng shui; the more food you show, the more "richness of life" you possess. Many fruits have special significance: you could choose apples to boost friendship, pears for energy, peaches for health and oranges for richness. You can include other favourite fruits as well.

Flowers are also a lovely decoration. Yellow ones are ideal to enhance communication. Silk, paper or plastic flowers are also fine. However, don't use dried flowers because they represent decay and stagnation.

location (see page 69). You can use coloured cloth and ceramics to represent different elements; for example, white represents metal, green signifies wood and yellow symbolizes earth. You can also enhance the "richness" with crystal glassware and with candles lit for the meal.

Lucky energy

The table and the area around it need to be "loaded with luck" (*chuang ho hsing yun*). To nurture goodness in the chi, have a few large, soft-leaved plants near the table if they suit the pa kua location. Pictures that give you feelings of pleasure and abundance will also help; good subjects include bright flowers, rounded fruit and sunny landscapes.

Keep electrical items, including TVs and stereos, out of the dining room; their energy is too yang. In addition, remove any clocks, because they are unwelcome reminders of the passing of time. A dining room should be "eternal" (*yung yuan te*).

Calming colours

The chi in a dining room needs to be more yin than yang, to help create a pleasant, relaxing feel. To stimulate yin chi, base the decor on pastel or neutral colours. For large areas such as walls, single colours are best. You can always use ornaments and pictures, or a display area with items that suit the pa kua location, to add splashes of brighter colours.

Try to avoid having highly patterned wallpaper, which can splinter the chi. If you already have this problem, remedy it by putting up abstract pictures in strong, plain colours appropriate for the pa kua location.

Lighting and mirrors

Lighting needs to be soft and calming. Wall-mounted lights equipped with dimmer switches are a good idea, because you can alter the lighting levels to suit your mood or a special occasion.

A mirror will also soften the light. Choose one with a suitable frame for that sector, or with bevelled edges. A large mirror reflecting the dining table and showing food such as a bowl of fruit will double "life wealth". However, a mirror should never reflect a kitchen or bathroom or it will double bad energy from these areas.

The water of life

Clean, flowing water symbolizes luck, energy, health and "richness of life". A small water feature or aquarium will benefit most pa kua locations. Alternatively, you could have one or two water symbols, such as shells, or a picture of flowing water. However, don't use water items in the northeast, south or southwest; they clash with the chi of these sectors.

Goldfish signify luck, and are ideal for an aquarium. Three or nine are the most beneficial numbers; include one black fish to represent protection. If you like tropical fish, have golden platys and a black mollie.

Special occasions

You can use lighting and décor to alter the energy and create different moods. For a family meal, or when you have guests, add plenty of light and colourful table settings to boost yang chi and encourage communication. For a romantic meal, choose dark or pastel-coloured table decorations, and low lighting or candles, to enhance yin energy.

Location, location, location

North: This sector governs career and progress; a dining room here is good for business guests. You can boost the chi with an ornament or picture symbolizing water; you can also include a landscape.

Northeast: The chi here can be too lively for a dining room. However, you can calm it by using earth symbols, such as crystal glassware.

East, southeast, south: These sectors have great energy for family dining rooms. In the east and southeast, blend wood symbols, such as plants and pictures of landscapes, with some water, such as a shell or a fish ornament. In the south, boost fire energy with reds and oranges, and with pictures of poppies, sunflowers, exotic birds or flamboyant rock stars.

Southwest, west: These locations make enjoyable chill-out areas. If you have a southwestern dining room and want to nurture your relationship with your partner, add pairs of brightly coloured candles or vases. To enhance chi in the west, opt for rounded vases or empty bowls in shiny metal. Adding crystal (earth) creates a helpful blend of energies.

Northwest: This dining room, in the "authority" sector, is ideal for business dinners. Rounded metal vases or bowls can enhance the chi.

水
火
不
宓

KITCHEN
Bitter rivals, angry neighbours

Kitchens are necessary rooms, but it can take a lot of work to produce the right blend of energies for them. The kitchen will always be a "yang" room, with lots of activity, but the sharp corners and electrical items in it may make the chi move too quickly. Another major problem is the clash of fire and water elements, such as the oven and the sink. In ancient feng shui, these conflicting elements were referred to as "bitter rivals, angry neighbours". The clash between them tends to divide and splinter the flow of chi.

The "alchemy" (*lien chin shu*) of feng shui will help you to control these potential problems. Generally, you need to balance the energy carefully to promote active, beneficial chi. This process involves using both the Constructive and Destructive Cycles of elements (see page 35). In addition, avoid disagreements in the kitchen, limit the number of sharp edges and try not to spend too much time there. Prepare the food and then go into your dining room or dining area to enjoy it.

The layout of your kitchen
The most important task is to assess the location of "fire" and "water" items in your kitchen. The oven, stove top (hob), microwave and toaster belong to the fire element, but the sink, fridge, freezer, washing machine and dishwasher belong to the water element. Water puts out fire.

The most auspicious layout is a triangle comprising the oven and stove top, sink and work surface; this layout prevents any clash of energies between the main fire and water items (see above right), and is practical because it will allow you to move easily between the three areas.

An ideal "triangle" layout

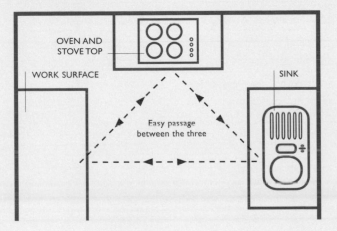

OVEN AND STOVE TOP

WORK SURFACE

SINK

Easy passage between the three

Another good layout is an oven and sink located on the same wall but separated by a work surface.

If you're planning a new kitchen, avoid placing fire and water appliances beside or opposite each other because their energies will clash; for example, don't have an oven opposite a fridge or beside a dishwasher.

Separating fire and water

Even if you can't redesign your kitchen, there are still various ways to separate fire and water energies. One method is by symbolically "pushing them apart" using light. If you have spotlights in the kitchen, point one at the water item and one at the fire item. In addition, you could direct a third spotlight at the kitchen door, to push the kitchen away from the rest of the house, or, if your kitchen has a dining area, point the light at this area to separate it from the rest of the room.

水
火
不
宜

Separating items that are side by side

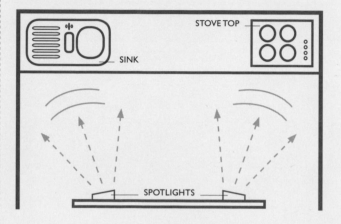

If your oven is opposite your sink, and your kitchen is large enough, you could separate the two items with an island unit, but choose one with a plain work surface; don't add a stove top to the unit, because the gas or electric rings form another fire symbol.

Separating items that face each other

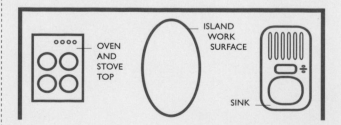

Another way to separate fire and water is to hide water items, such as a fridge-freezer, behind the doors of your kitchen cabinets. ("Hide it and it disappears" is a handy basic rule in feng shui.) Simplest of all, you can lay a thin, non-slip rug or runner, in a plain colour that suits the pa kua location, between the conflicting items.

Areas for eating

If possible, eat in a separate dining room, where the energy will nurture feelings of calm and "richness of life" (see page 62). Try to avoid having meals in the kitchen, where the chi is too strong and fast-moving to encourage good digestion. However, if you don't have a dining room, you can still create a separate dining area in the kitchen by marking the space off with kitchen cabinets or furniture (see page 63), and using colours and materials that promote calming energy.

Choosing colours

Clever use of colours is the easiest way to blend energies in a kitchen. Use just two or three main colours so you don't over-stimulate the chi. Light colours on the walls are enlivening without being too powerful. If you wish, you can add a few stronger touches with equipment and utensils that suit the pa kua location (see page 79).

Lighting and reflections

To freshen the chi and help it to circulate, you need plenty of natural and artificial light. Halogen lights set into the ceiling are ideal because they cast almost no shadow. Racks of three or five spotlights are also excellent. However, avoid neon lights; their energy is too harsh and the flickering can cause headaches. If you have neon lights that you can't remove, include lots of rounded shapes (see page 74) to soften the energy.

水火不宣

Never use mirrors in kitchens, because they will reflect the energy of the "dead" food and double it. If you need reflective surfaces for your pa kua location, you could use shiny, rounded stainless steel or chrome utensils. These items reflect their surroundings, but because they distort the image, they don't cause the problems that mirrors would do.

Surfaces and corners

Help the chi to flow freely by keeping work surfaces clear. Don't leave dirty plates or clutter around – the mess will attract stagnant chi that can enter food. If you need to keep items such as kettles, toasters or coffee machines on the work surface, push them toward the back.

The sharp edges in a kitchen stimulate yang chi, but too many can cause tension and arguments between people (or, as I once heard it described, "bitchin' in the kitchen"). Balance them with rounded corners on kitchen cabinets and work surfaces, and round, shiny utensils, to help the chi curve and meander. If your cabinets have sharp corners, fit lights under and inside the top ones and keep the lights on while you work.

Storing equipment

Store equipment in kitchen cabinets, or stack it neatly, when you're not using it. However, if you have an oven in a bad pa kua location you can hang metal saucepans above or near it to deflect the fire energy. Keep knives in a knife block and scissors in a drawer. If possible, don't have these sharp implements on display because they give out harmful chi.

Electrical appliances

The electromagnetic energy from objects such as blenders, kettles and toasters contributes to yang chi. However, as with the TV and stereo in the living room (see page 60), you can actually use these pieces of electrical equipment to increase beneficial yang chi (see page 60). Keep the items in good condition so they work safely and efficiently, and make sure they work quietly so they give out good chi.

Positioning microwave ovens

Microwave ovens emit electromagnetic energy, which is seen as harmful in feng shui (see page 127). Don't use a microwave if you can avoid it, or else use it as little as possible. To control its energy, put it in a corner ruled by fire. (Microwaves are usually made of shiny metal, which symbolizes water and "puts out" fire.) Otherwise, hide it inside a cabinet. If you're planning a new kitchen, build the microwave into the surrounding cabinets so only the face is showing.

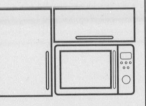

Planning meals

The colours and tastes of foods can produce different blends of yin and yang chi. Brightly coloured foods are yang; green vegetables are a balance of yin and yang; and white foods, such as dairy products, are yin. You can plan each course of a meal to have its own energy. For example, a starter is usually yang, a main course is often a mix and a dessert will be yin.

Relaxing, intimate meals need more yin chi, while parties and business lunches or dinners need more yang. For a children's party, you could start with activities, then offer calming yin food; try to avoid bright colours and cooked meats, which would be too yang.

Preparing food

The kitchen has very negative chi because of the meat, fruit and vegetables prepared there. Once the ingredients have been turned into food they become lucky, but food being prepared, and even the smell of it, is bad feng shui. Keep the kitchen door closed as much as possible, so strong food smells don't escape and pervade the whole house. In addition, make sure that people can't see into a kitchen from the front door or from other rooms.

Herbal remedies

Fresh herbs in little pots, for immediate use, stimulate beneficial chi, because herbs are nourishing foodstuffs. Buy them regularly from your local supermarket, and keep them on the window sill, until needed; the herbs will also absorb good chi through the window. If your kitchen is connected to your dining room, fragrant herbs are good for taking away smells and stagnant or even toxic energy from food preparation.

If you wish to grow herbs yourself, however, keep them outside. Never have auspicious items, such as potted plants (or lucky ornaments, or pets' beds) in a kitchen, because the good luck that they give out will be lost within the bad energy of the room.

Protecting beds above kitchens

If your kitchen is under a bedroom, check that you don't have any beds directly above the oven. The heat from the stove top will "cook" or "burn" the inner chi of anyone who has to sleep regularly in that bed, attacking the immune system and bringing on niggling infections, colds, coughs, sore throats and headaches.

The best solution is to move the bed or the oven. If you can't do this, lay a silver-painted or foil-covered board under the bed, with the shiny side facing downward. The board just needs to be long enough to protect the sleeper's head and chest. In the kitchen, you can use lots of shiny, rounded metal, such as stainless-steel and chrome pans, filled with water and left on the stove top overnight. If you have a stainless-steel hood above the stove top, this is also helpful. In each case, the shiny, reflective metal represents water and will "put out the fire".

Working with elemental energies

In ancient China, kitchens were located in the east sector (wood) or the southeast sector (wood, with touches of water and wind). The most favoured was the southeast, where the breezes were considered to "help keep the charcoal stove alight". The southeast also symbolizes "richness of life": prosperity, health and satisfying family relationships.

The table overleaf shows how fire and water fit into each pa kua location. The east and southeast can support these energies, so they're ideal for a kitchen. However, the other locations support only fire, only water or neither, so you need to blend the energies more carefully.

DOCTOR'S ORDERS

Problem: A fire item is in a pa kua sector ruled by water, or vice versa, and you can't reposition it.

Remedy: Bring in other elements to stop the conflict. If you have an oven in the north, use shiny metals to destroy the water energy. If you have a sink in the south, surround it with earth colours or symbols, which "soak up" the water; choose warm, earthy colours for the walls, granite or marble work surfaces, and stone or terracotta tiles above a sink.

ROOM BY ROOM

水
火
不
容

MANAGING FIRE AND WATER ENERGIES			
SECTOR	RULING ELEMENT	SUPPORTS FIRE	SUPPORTS WATER
North	Water	No	Yes
Northeast	Earth	Yes	No
East	Wood	Yes	Yes
Southeast	Wood	Yes	Yes
South	Fire	Yes	No
Southwest	Earth	Yes	No
West	Metal	No	Yes
Northwest	Metal	No	Yes

If you have wooden cabinets in a pa kua location that doesn't suit wood, you can still benefit from the wood's energy by painting them to go with that sector (see opposite) or choosing a suitable colour of wood.

When you paint wood (or any surface) it takes on the elemental energy symbolized by that colour; the colour on the surface overcomes the energy of the wood beneath. For example, white-painted wood "becomes" metal. The natural colour of the wood can also help. Pine and oak symbolize wood, but maple is so pale that it symbolizes metal, and cherry represents earth. With regard to flooring, you can use tiles, vinyl or wood, depending on the pa kua location.

Controlling energy in a utility room

If you have a utility room next to your kitchen, the water energy can drain energy from the rest of the house, as in a bathroom (see page 80). To control the problem, use earth symbols, such as warm yellows, apricot or caramel colours for walls and terracotta or stone tiling.

Location, location, location

North: The most beneficial elements in a northern kitchen are wood and metal, because water supports both of them in the Constructive Cycle of elements (see page 35). Metallic colours and white, Shaker-style kitchens, and wooden surfaces and flooring are good choices.

Northeast: A blend of earth and metal works well here. Good choices include warm, earthy colours such as oatmeal and caramel for walls; terracotta or stone flooring; granite or marble work surfaces; and shiny pans and utensils in stainless steel, chrome, copper or brass.

East: The east is governed by the wood element, so wooden surfaces, and "wood" colours such as green, are best in eastern kitchens. Yellows and reds also promote helpful energy.

Southeast: The most auspicious location of all for a kitchen, the southeast is ruled by the wood element, so wooden surfaces and "wood" colours (see East, above) work especially well here.

South: Wood and earth symbols are beneficial in a southern kitchen, because these elements support fire, the ruling element of the south. Wooden cupboards and floors, earthy colours, terracotta or stone flooring and wood or granite work surfaces all go well here.

Southwest, west, northwest: For kitchens in these sectors, shiny metal with warm earth will form a rich blend. Metal colours (white, cream, silver-grey) and/or rounded metal utensils bring in beneficial energies. Earthy colours such as caramel and oatmeal, terracotta or stone flooring and granite or marble work surfaces would also be good choices.

气
泡

BATHROOM
Energy drain

Clean, pure, flowing water represents good yang chi, power and "richness of life" (*ts'ai fu*). However, watery rooms such as bathrooms and utility rooms need particularly careful treatment in feng shui. In these rooms, we constantly make the water filthy as we use it. As the dirty water is discharged, the chi in your home is polluted and then lost, draining protection and energy from the building and possibly from you. This process is literally called a "drain" (*kou chu*). However, you can easily control the problem so you get the most from your bathroom.

A healthy bathroom
Your most powerful tool for stopping the drain of energy is the earth element. In the Destructive Cycle of elements (see page 35), earth blocks and absorbs water, just as blotting paper absorbs ink. Earth colours and accessories (see page 83) also control the water's yang chi so the energy is strong but not overpowering.

The chi of a bathroom should be slightly more yang than yin. To promote "richness of life" without using water, choose rounded shapes for fixtures such as bathtubs and sinks, and accessories such as mirrors (see page 85). These shapes also keep the flow of chi "measured and meandering". Avoid straight edges if possible – they speed up the chi.

The layout of your bathroom

If you're planning a new bathroom, try to arrange it so the toilet, sink and plughole (drain) for the bath are all positioned against the same wall. This arrangement concentrates all the draining energy

A well organized bathroom

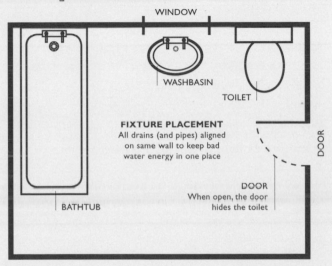

WINDOW

WASHBASIN

TOILET

FIXTURE PLACEMENT
All drains (and pipes) aligned
on same wall to keep bad
water energy in one place

DOOR

DOOR
When open, the door
hides the toilet

BATHTUB

in one area. It also strengthens the other walls, which is an advantage if you have a bedroom or office on the other side of these walls.

In addition, hide the toilet in a recess or behind the door if you can, so it's never the first thing you see on entering the bathroom. (If you've ever been to the bathroom in someone else's house and had to spend a few moments looking for the toilet, that's the effect to aim for.) Remember to keep the bathroom door shut to protect the rest of the house from the draining energy in the room.

If the bathroom is above your kitchen, try to avoid having the toilet over the oven because the toilet's water energy will clash with the oven's fire energy (see page 77). If you already have a toilet here, use earthy flooring such as terracotta, limestone or slate; its energy will block the water.

气
池

The benefits of wet rooms

Wet rooms (walk-in showers), which are becoming increasingly popular, are actually beneficial in feng shui terms because they let dirty water drain away immediately while you're washing, as opposed to baths and shower trays, which hold on to the water. If you're planning to build a wet room, choose surfacing and non-slip flooring that symbolizes earth, such as limestone, slate, granite or terracotta.

The power of light

Natural light is important in a bathroom because it helps to stabilize and freshen the chi. Often, however, especially with small toilet rooms, there are no windows at all. In any bathroom, especially one with no windows, you need good lighting. Ceiling-mounted halogen lights minimize shadows, while spotlight racks of three or five lights can be

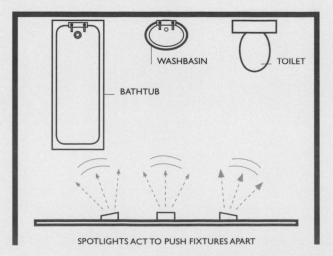

WASHBASIN

TOILET

BATHTUB

SPOTLIGHTS ACT TO PUSH FIXTURES APART

used to correct problem areas. Point the spotlights at the door, toilet, sink, bathtub and shower, symbolically "pushing them apart" and thus reducing their power on the energy of the room.

Perfect plumbing

Keep your bathroom fixtures in good condition and fix any plumbing problems, such as dripping water or leaks. Aside from the practical benefits, getting a plumber in is a worthwhile investment for feng shui because it will help to stop any needless outflow of energy.

Earthy colours

Use earth colours and symbols throughout the bathroom. Earthy colours give a warm, welcoming feel, and will give the strong protection you need to stop chi from being distorted and drained away.

For walls, tiling, flooring and fixtures, choose colours such as yellow, terracotta, caramel, stone, pink, peach, apricot and plum. Even accessories such as face cloths, bathrobes, towels and shower curtains in these colours will be helpful. If you wish to use patterns, keep them as simple as possible, and limit yourself to two or three main colours. Get the colours right and you'll feel the warmth.

Protective accessories

An especially good way to stimulate beneficial earth energy is to decorate your bathroom with earthy accessories. You could have stone or terracotta dishes or pots, filled with pretty, rounded pebbles, and nightlights and candles in earthy colours. You can also place attractive pebbles in plugholes, when a bathtub or basin is not in use, to prevent small losses of energy; just choose pebbles large enough not to slip down the drain. Often, in feng shui, you're told that plugs should be placed in plugholes, but pebbles do the job much better. If you develop a leaky tap (faucet) when you're not at home, the pebble will still allow water to flow away, but a plug will let stagnant water collect.

The power of scent

Using pleasant scents can stimulate the chi in a bathroom, and is a quick and easy way to make yourself feel uplifted or, conversely, relaxed. Scented candles provide soft light to add to the atmosphere. Alternatively, and for a more lasting effect, you could have a bowl of scented stones. Lavender and citrus scents are beneficial because they symbolize earth. Patchouli

is also good because it has a purifying effect. However, don't use pine or sandalwood, because they belong to the wood element, and also avoid floral scents, because they have very fiery energy.

Stay away from the seashore!

If you use "watery" symbols and decorations in your bathroom, you'll add to the yin energy and aggravate the problems. The classic blue bathroom, with lots of shells, dolphins, crabs, starfish, killer whales, fishing boats, frogs, fishing nets, divers, and so on – what I call the "undersea world of Jacques Cousteau" – is best avoided if possible.

The colour blue is a symbol of water, so you should really try to keep it out of rooms that are already over-dominated by water. (Indeed, think carefully wherever you use blue; apply it in splashes and small touches, rather than over large areas.) Blue can sometimes be a cold, unwelcoming colour, and a bathroom can be a cold room anyway, especially first thing on a winter morning, without adding to the effect.

Using wood and metal

Many people have plants and wooden cabinets or other furniture in their bathrooms. However, you should beware of using wood, because wood supports water in the Constructive Cycle of elements, so it will actually increase the bad effects of the nasty water. Replace wood symbols with earth symbols, or paint any fixed wooden items in earth colours; the wood, when painted, will take on the element symbolized by the colour of the paint. Metal colours, such as white or silver, have a neutral effect in bathrooms — but they can give a rather cold feel, so balance them with earth symbols.

Mirrors

Mirrors in bathrooms can increase light, but they also symbolize water and can worsen the draining energy. Have the smallest mirror that will serve your needs, with a frame or a bevelled edge to control the water energy. Hang it so it won't reflect a toilet or bidet and fix it at the height of the tallest person in your house, so it won't "cut off" the top of his or her head. Avoid mirror tiles, because their edges chop up the chi.

"Hiding" the bathroom

Hanging a mirror on the outside of a bathroom door effectively makes the room "disappear" and will help to stop the bathroom from draining energy out of the house. Using a mirror is a particularly good idea if the bathroom is beside or facing a front or back door, or a bedroom, kitchen, study or office door.

You can also "hide" the bathroom by keeping the door closed at all times. If you have an en-suite bathroom with no door, either add a door or, if this is not possible, hang a curtain over the entrance to separate the bathroom from the bedroom.

Controlling energy loss

It has often been said that flushing the toilet equals "flushing away wealth". More accurately, the flow of dirty water down a toilet pulls the chi away from the rest of the home (see page 80). To stop this energy drain, close the toilet lid before you flush, and keep the lid down at all other times.

For extra protection, a traditional feng shui method to suppress the draining effect of a toilet is to hang a small, unobtrusive wind chime with five solid metal bars above it. The bars push energy down into the toilet. If this remedy is not to your taste, simply use earth colours as described on previous pages, and place a bowl or pot of decorative pebbles close to the toilet, to reduce this downward pull of energy.

DOCTOR'S ORDERS

Problem: You have a bathroom in a bad location, such as beside or opposite the front door or facing the back door.
Remedy: Block the draining effect of the water immediately by using warm, rich earth colours in the bathroom. Keep the door closed. If your bathroom is on the left-hand side of the front door (as you face the door from inside), hang a mirror on the bathroom door to "hide" the room.

Enhancing bathrooms in any pa kua sector

Bathrooms can easily drain the energies of any pa kua location. For a bathroom in any sector, the solution is to add earth colours to block the drainage of energy. You can also use metal, but avoid fire, wood and, in particular, adding more water symbols.

Location, location, location

North: You need to be especially careful with a bathroom in the north, because this location is already governed by water, so the water energy is likely to be overpowering.

Northeast: This is one of the best possible locations for a bathroom, because it is governed by earth, which will help to control the energy of the water.

East, southeast: These two sectors are governed by wood, which supports water and will actually increase the draining energy.

South: This sector is ruled by fire, which clashes with water. Using earth symbols will help to control both of these elements.

Southwest: Like the northeast, this sector is ruled by earth, so is one of the better choices for a bathroom.

West, northwest: These two sectors, whose ruling element is metal, are also among the "least worst" choices for bathrooms.

BEDROOM
Rest

Your bedroom should be a place of sanctuary. The Chinese called it "the snake's nest ... the sun's rest" (*ch'ao ... jih lo*). The snake is a symbol of health and energy and nests in safe, secluded places. The "sun's rest" is night, when yin chi (see page 32) reaches its peak. You need to create a blend that's strongly yin with some yang, to recharge your inner chi.

Laying out your bedroom

If possible, place your bed with the headboard against a solid wall (one with no window or door). When you're in bed, you should ideally have a clear view of the door and windows. However, it's very bad luck to have your feet pointing directly at a window or door. This is traditionally known as the "corpse" position, and in ancient China was the position in which a dead body was laid before being carried from the home.

Ideally, there should be only one door into a bedroom and no more than three windows. If you have too many doors or windows they can

---

DOCTOR'S ORDERS

Problem: Your bed is directly in line with a door or window.

Remedy: Break the line between the bed and the door or window by placing a chest of drawers or a dressing table at the foot of the bed; use one a little higher than the window sill if the bed is opposite a window. A sleigh bed can also help, because it has a high footboard.

A restful sanctuary

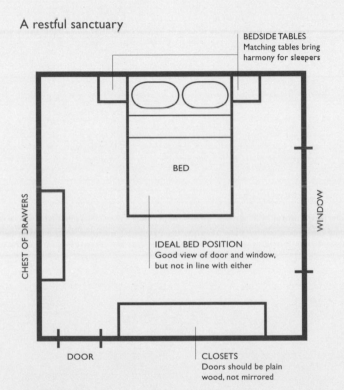

BEDSIDE TABLES
Matching tables bring harmony for sleepers

BED

CHEST OF DRAWERS

WINDOW

IDEAL BED POSITION
Good view of door and window, but not in line with either

DOOR

CLOSETS
Doors should be plain wood, not mirrored

let in disturbing energy, and you'll need to calm the chi with yin items such as thick, plush curtains, soft pillows and pastel or dark bedlinen.

Check that the windows don't look onto "poison arrows" (see pages 126–7), such as the ends of roofs, which will aim harmful chi at the room. To ward off a poison arrow, you can place a crystal ornament in the window, or have a strong, protective animal figure – such as a picture of a dog or lion, or a teddy bear – on the window sill, facing the arrow.

Controlling chi from bathrooms

Many people have an en-suite bathroom for comfort and conven-
ience, but it contains "filthy" water, which drains your chi (see page 80).
Control the draining water energy with earth colours and symbols (see
page 83) and keep the door closed. You can also protect your bed by
having a dressing area between your bed and the bathroom.

En-suite bathrooms that project into a bedroom can form alcoves,
which generate stagnant chi (see page 55). To solve the problem, fill the
alcove with a wardrobe, dressing table or chest of drawers.

Selecting comfortable beds

Choose a bed that fits your room comfortably. Make sure children's
beds are big enough for them as they grow. It's better to have a divan
or a bed with legs, but avoid bunk beds because the person in the lower
one is boxed in, while the one on top is squashed against the ceiling. This
can depress the chi of both sleepers. Low beds such as futons expose
you to stagnant chi at ground level, making you lethargic; to lift the chi,
put lights around the bed, or try using brighter-coloured bedlinen.

Sleigh beds protect your head and feet, and their curving shape
promotes gently flowing chi. Four-poster beds and "princess" beds are
also beneficial, because their canopies protect you and enliven the chi
around the bed. A four-poster is especially good if a ceiling has beams;
the canopy counteracts the downward energy from the beams.

Protecting your head

If possible, have a solid wooden headboard. In feng shui, the headboard
is thought to be like a traditional Chinese gravestone, which protects the
energy at the top of a person's head. Rectangular headboards stabilize
chi, while headboards with rounded tops help chi to circulate.

Try not to have cupboards or shelves above a bed; these are seen as "slicing blades" (*tao p'ien*), trapping you in a box of stagnant chi. If you can't remove them, install uplighters on the wall beneath (or under a top bunk, if you have bunk beds), or put a lava lamp by the bed, to lift the chi. In addition, fit a timer switch so the main lights come on two hours before bedtime.

Calm and cosy decor

To enhance yin chi and quieten the feel of the room, use pale, pastel or dark colours; bright, mid-toned colours are more yang. Choose thick, soft, plush furnishings and furniture with rounded edges, which are more yin. (Thinner, firmer, straight-edged furnishings are more yang.)

You need richer colours for bedlinen than for floors, walls or curtains, because these colours enclose you in a stable energy field as you sleep. If you like, have different sets of bedlinen to change the mood of the bedroom; however, stick to plain colours or large, simple patterns.

Try to keep pictures and ornaments to a minimum, to ensure a peaceful environment. Avoid having pictures hanging over your head, because they hold stagnant energy that pushes down on you; they could also fall on you. It's best not to keep plants in the room unless someone is ill, because their energy is too stimulating for bedrooms.

Mirrors and TVs

During the night, the most "yin" time, you emit worn-out chi while you sleep and absorb fresh supplies. If you have a mirror reflecting you in bed, it will bounce some of that worn-out chi back at you. Ancient feng shui masters also said the mirror would "put a third person in the bed", which is extremely bad for relationships.

休
息

To protect your energy, cover mirrors or tilt them away from you at night. If you have a TV in your room, bear in mind that the screen will turn into a mirror when you switch it off, so turn it away from the bed, or cover it with a cloth once it has cooled.

Electricity in the bedroom

If possible, keep electrical items away from the bed, except for small bedside lamps, because electricity can disturb your inner chi while you sleep. It's best not to have a TV in the bedroom, and certainly not close to the bed. Wiring and appliances can produce surges of electricity, and static charges may remain when appliances have been switched off.

Ideally, have a wooden bed and headboard, because wood doesn't conduct electricity or hold static charges. You can paint the wood to fit your decor or the pa kua sector (see page 78). Try to avoid metal beds, because metal conducts static electricity. A water bed is especially bad because water and electricity can both disrupt your inner chi.

DOCTOR'S ORDERS

Problem: *You have a metal bed and you can't replace it.*
Remedy: Wrap natural fabric such as cotton or silk around the bed frame to reduce the charge of static electricity from it. Yellow (symbolizing earth) or green (wood) are the best colours for the fabric.

To reduce the harmful effects of electricity, use earthy colours such as terracotta or peach for bedlinen, if they suit the pa kua location, or have a battery-powered clock or a wind-up radio instead of electrical ones.

Storing clothes neatly

Keep the room's energy clear by putting clothes away neatly. Put dirty clothes in a laundry bag or bin with a lid, preferably in a bathroom or utility room. Put any clothes that you're not using into storage.

Nourishing relationships

If you share a bed, try to place it so you and your partner can use both sides freely, to ensure balance and harmony. If you have one side of the bed pushed against a wall, the person who can get in and out most

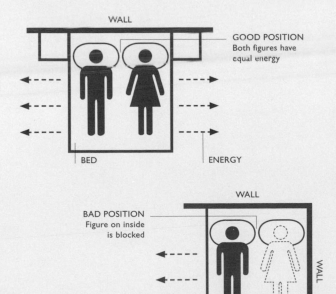

休息

easily will dominate the energy of the room. In addition, place matching bedside tables, lamps and rugs on each side of the bed; this will also help to equalize the energies.

Children's bedrooms

Children need space for activities and study as well as sleep. Divide their bedrooms into three areas, with different blends of yin and yang. Sleep areas should be yin, with quiet colours; other areas need to be yang, with brighter colours and lots of light. The correct blend also depends on your child; pastel colours can help to calm hyperactive children, while brighter or earthy colours can boost confidence in shy children.

The uses will change over time. For example, young children might use their activity area for toys, but older ones might use it for hobbies. Students may find this layout helpful for study/bedrooms at college.

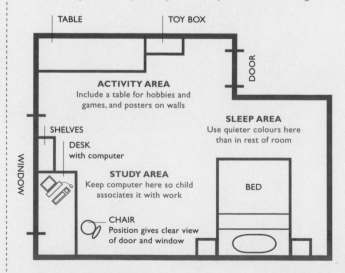

Location, location, location

North: The relaxing water energy in a northern bedroom is ideal for sleep. Good colours are black, as well as the metal colours white, cream, grey, gold and silver. You could also use wood symbols, such as touches of pale green and wooden furniture. A wooden floor is ideal here.

Northeast: Try to avoid having bedrooms here, because the chi is too disturbing for sleep. If just part of the room lies in the northeast, use the space for meditation, yoga or exercise, or as a dressing area. If you have to sleep here, have curtains and bedlinen in light earth colours such as pink, peach, oatmeal or pale yellow to stabilize sleep patterns.

East, southeast, south: The chi in these sectors is very nourishing for sleep. Choose from pale greens (wood), pale yellows, pinks and lilacs (earth), all of which provide calming energy. Wooden floors are excellent for these bedrooms.

Southwest: If you have a bedroom in the southwest and wish to enhance your relationship with your partner, have pictures showing just the two of you. Generally, though, the chi is too sluggish for a bedroom. A mixture of pastels, brighter earth colours and metal colours such as white, cream or grey, can lift and stabilize the energy.

West, northwest: The northwest is the site of authority – ideal for a parents' bedroom. It's best not to have guests' or children's rooms here, as this would risk you "giving away" your power. A western bedroom, symbolizing children, is ideal for couples wanting a baby. In both sectors, a mixture of metal and earth works best. Avoid fiery colours. If you have wooden floors, cover them with rugs in metal or earth colours.

阳
阴
乎
衡

EXTRA ROOMS
Balancing energy

Building extra rooms onto your house can be a good way to increase living space and add to the value of your property. You could enlarge your home outward, with an extension or conservatory (sun room), or upward, by converting an attic or roof space into a loft room.

Any extra space should always have a definite function, not merely be a dumping ground for clutter. By defining the function you can improve the flow of chi in this new area. Try to create a blend of chi that suits the room's use. Whatever the blend, keep the space neat to produce an ideal, "measured and meandering" flow of chi.

Laying out an extension or conservatory (sun room)

The size and shape of an extension, and the pa kua sectors that it covers, will determine its energy. Angular shapes are more yang, and their lively energy would be ideal for a work or activity room. Rounded shapes are more yin, and would suit a room for relaxation or a play-room. Conservatories are usually places for relaxing, so need to be more yin; curved shapes would therefore be better for these areas.

Make a plan of your home including the extra space, or use the initial plans if you're having a new extension or conversion, and work out which pa kua sectors the planned areas will occupy (see page 19).

A small extension, such as a conservatory, can enable you to utilize more of the energy of the pa kua sector that it occupies, and by using the space you'll stimulate the chi. However, some extensions can form "missing areas"; see opposite (and pages 16–17). To avoid having these areas, run your extension along the whole side of the building. If you

Making the most of conservatory shapes

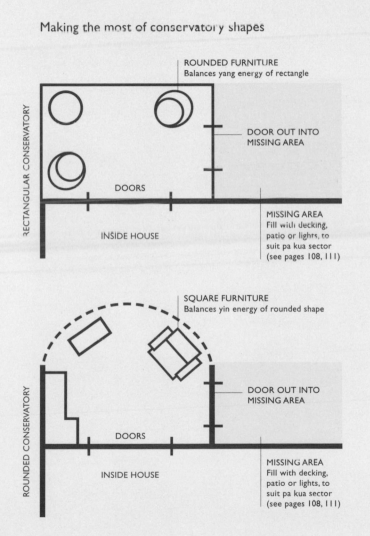

ROUNDED FURNITURE
Balances yang energy of rectangle

RECTANGULAR CONSERVATORY

DOOR OUT INTO
MISSING AREA

DOORS

INSIDE HOUSE

MISSING AREA
Fill with decking,
patio or lights, to
suit pa kua sector
(see pages 108, 111)

SQUARE FURNITURE
Balances yin energy of rounded shape

ROUNDED CONSERVATORY

DOOR OUT INTO
MISSING AREA

DOORS

INSIDE HOUSE

MISSING AREA
Fill with decking,
patio or lights, to
suit pa kua sector
(see pages 108, 111)

already have a missing area, "fill it in" by making it into a patio, or add lights and plants to suit the pa kua location (see pages 108 and 111).

You also need to check the position of the outer and inner doors. If both doors are in line, chi can rush out of the house. It's best to have them at right angles to each other. If you have a missing area, an outer door leading into the area will help to "fill it in" (see page 97).

DOCTOR'S ORDERS

Problem: *Your extension has the outside and inside doors directly in line, which allows the chi to rush through too fast.*

Remedy: To slow the chi, put a large plant or a rounded rug in a suitable colour by one of the doors, depending on the pa kua sector (see pages 143–5). If a planned extension forms a missing area, have the outer door leading into the area.

Rebalancing the centre of your home

A large extension or conservatory will move the *tai chi* (central point), or "earthpot", which you found when drawing the plans of your home (see page 16), so you'll have to redraw these plans to include it.

It's best to have the *tai chi* within a property, and you need to keep it clear. Moving the *tai chi* can help to enhance pa kua sectors. However, if the *tai chi* moves too far from the original centre, the building's energy may become unbalanced – like a badly laden boat with all the weight at one end. If the *tai chi* is in a cupboard or alcove, the chi will be blocked. You'll need to stimulate it by painting the interior an earthy colour (such as yellow or oatmeal), keeping a light on in or near the area for a few hours each day, or having a telephone or computer there.

In some cases, the *tai chi* moves outside the building altogether, which severely unbalances the property's energy. This often happens if a building is an "L" shape, known in feng shui as a "meat cleaver" (*fu*). To combat the problem, fill in the missing area as suggested opposite. Add earth colours and symbols around the *tai chi* to enhance its earth energy.

Creating a loft

Opening up your roof space to create a loft can be a great asset, as long as you organize the space carefully. Sloping ceilings in lofts can be a problem. The slope slows the chi, squashes it and quickly turns it yin and stagnant. If part of your loft has a sloping ceiling that you can't stand up in, use the space as a wardrobe or storage area, and use the full height

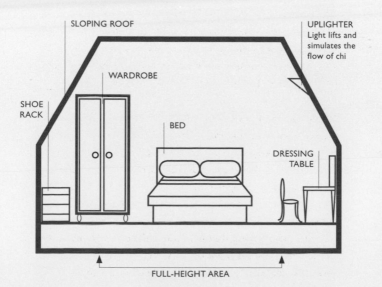

SLOPING ROOF

UPLIGHTER
Light lifts and
simulates the
flow of chi

WARDROBE

SHOE
RACK

BED

DRESSING
TABLE

FULL-HEIGHT AREA

area for work or sleeping. If you have no choice, put an uplighter or a lava lamp under the slope to lift the energy. In children's rooms, you could use decorative mobiles and small lights in the same way.

Planning a home office

An office or other work space in a home will be covered in much more detail in the next chapter, but since home offices are becoming more and more popular and a common use for an extension or loft, I thought I would mention a few of the basic points here.

An office should look and function like an office and only contain items relating to work. To keep the energy focused, try not to combine it with other areas, such as a bedroom, nursery or storage room. If this is unavoidable, separate the work space from these other areas by using a screen or some pieces of furniture.

In a work space, yang energy should outbalance yin to bring strength, power and activity. Vertical blinds at windows are a good way to lift the energy in the room. A desk needs a clear view of the door, but should not directly face it because this position can make you insecure.

Providing good access to a loft

Another important consideration for lofts is staircase access. Make sure the stairs will be easy to use and not too steep. Try to avoid having stairs that "confront", or face, a bathroom door, because chi can rush down the stairs and drain away through the bathroom. If you already have stairs in this position, put a rounded, non-slip rug (in a suitable colour for the pa kua location) at the bottom to steady the flow of chi.

Don't choose a spiral staircase, because the chi rushes down and between the steps and is wasted. However, if you already have one, there are various ways you can conserve the chi (see page 52).

Decorating the room

First, you need to set your intention for the space: are you going to use it for activities, or would you prefer a quiet area? If you want to boost yang energy for activities, choose furniture with square or rectangular shapes. To enhance yin energy, use soft, rounded, plush furnishings, such as soft cushions and thick curtains.

If you have an angular conservatory, balance the energies by adding rounded furnishings (see page 97). Keep furniture to a minimum, and choose plain colours or simple patterns to provide calming chi.

Balancing the energies

In many cases, extensions or lofts occupy two or three pa kua sectors. You may find that the colour of walls or floors is right for one sector but wrong for another. You can, however, fix this problem by following the ABC of feng shui – awareness, balance and control (see page 40).

First, identify the elements you need in that sector. Then, if you find any wrong ones, simply lay the correct elemental colour or symbol on top to balance it out. Think of it as adding a bandage to a wound. In ancient feng shui, the correct colour was said to "sit on top" (ma pei: literally, "on the horse's back"). You can use the same technique in a conservatory whose walls have a lot of glass.

Correcting clashes between elements

If you have tiles (symbolizing earth) in a sector that doesn't suit earth, add symbols of wood, because wood destroys earth in the Destructive Cycle of elements (see page 35). You could have wooden, rattan or cane furniture, with green, red or yellow cushions, or put down non-slip rugs in these colours. Large evergreen plants in wooden tubs or in green, red or yellow pots are another way of achieving the correct blend.

阳
阴
乎
衡

If a wooden floor is in the wrong pa kua sector for wood, add metal or earth symbols to control its energy. For metal, have furniture or rugs in white, cream, grey, silver or gold. For earth, you could choose soft furnishings in earthy colours such as terracotta, caramel and oatmeal.

If you have a conservatory in the wrong sector for plants, there are various ways you can control the wood energy of the plants. West and northwest are the most challenging sectors, because they're governed by metal and metal destroys wood. In this case, choose plants with grey, white or silver leaves, to promote metal energy, or have metal pots. You could also use earth symbols such as ceramic or terracotta pots, or pebbles laid on the soil.

Plants may not suit an earth sector (northeast or southwest) because wood destroys earth. To harmonize the energies, you could use "metal" plant colours as described above, combine metal and earth symbols, or boost fire energy by hanging fairy lights around the plants.

Making use of garage space

If you have a car, keep the garage clear so the car is the only thing in it. Cars have strong metal and fire energies; if you have a room above your garage, the car can actually boost and stabilize the chi there. If you use your garage for any other purpose, such as storage (see below), be clear about this purpose and keep the space clean and well organized.

Storing equipment neatly

Ideally, keep all storage in a separate room. If you have shelves, the horizontal lines of their edges will give out harmful chi; to remedy the problem, hide the edges behind a cupboard door. Alternatively, place items such as books or manuals vertically, with their spines overlapping the shelf edges. If you have a work bench, keep it neat.

Location, location, location

North: A northern room is good for an office or study.

Northeast: This sector is ideal for physical activities, or activities with some spiritual content. Possible uses include a home gym, a meditation room, a room for yoga, or a space for martial arts, t'ai chi or chi kung.

East: The uplifting energy is lovely for a breakfast room or family room. The east is ruled by wood, which is ideal for a conservatory.

Southeast: This sector is ideal for a general office or for dealing with family finances. The wood energy is wonderful for a conservatory.

South: This sector is beneficial for communications and social activities, because it promotes connections to the outside world.

Southwest: This is a space for couples. If you have a family, try to keep it just for yourself and your partner, to nourish your relationship. The sluggish, relaxing chi here won't suit an office or business.

West: The chi in the west is ideal for creative activities, and also supports children's rooms, but it's just as good for quieter hobbies and relaxing. If you have a hectic life and wish to include more yin energy in your home, have a chill-out area or conservatory in the west.

Northwest: The northwest is the natural location for authority, so is ideal for a parent's study or an office. However, this is not a good place for a children's room because you will be "giving away" the authority position, so the children may tend to dominate the house.

曲线与色彩

GARDEN OR BACKYARD
Curves and colours

Originally, in ancient China, feng shui was used for choosing grave sites, crops and planting, and positioning homes (see page 23). Therefore, gardens or back yards are important spaces in feng shui. Classical feng shui gardens are asymmetrical, and the centre (the *tai chi*) is left clear. However, you can have any style of garden – an English cottage garden, a Mediterranean-style garden, a formal courtyard, or a simple back yard with some pots – and still apply feng shui effectively.

Think of your garden as an extension of your house (within the same pa kua). By using feng shui, you can connect the energies of the indoors and the outdoors. The chi from your garden will flow through your house, complementing the energies within your home.

Laying out your garden

First, you need to set your intention for the garden: define who will be using it and what you want to use it for. Then decide on the mix of yin and yang energy (see page 32) you prefer. Different areas can be suitable for different purposes. The chi of a feng shui garden is usually yin: relaxing (*sung chih*) and stress-free. However, most gardens also have pockets where yang energy is more to the fore; these areas are better for socializing and family activities.

For paths and flowerbeds, meandering curves are better than straight lines. As well as being more pleasing to the eye, curves let chi circulate gently, without rushing through the garden and being wasted. They are also protective; Chinese tradition teaches that devils and evil spirits travel in straight lines and can't go around bends!

An auspicious garden layout

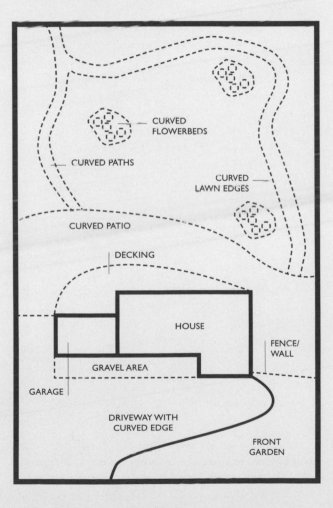

CURVED
FLOWERBEDS

CURVED PATHS

CURVED
LAWN EDGES

CURVED PATIO

DECKING

HOUSE

FENCE/
WALL

GRAVEL AREA

GARAGE

DRIVEWAY WITH
CURVED EDGE

FRONT
GARDEN

曲
线
与
色
彩

Protecting the garden

To get the most from your garden's energies, you need to make sure that plenty of good chi enters it from outside, and minimize the amount of harmful chi coming in. Look for any possible sources of problems (see pages 126–8), particularly "poison arrows", which produce rushing chi that hits your home violently. If you have any of these problems, use plants or fencing to protect your home (see opposite).

If you have problems with noise or disagreeable neighbours, you can protect your boundary with bamboo; *Phyllostachys* and/or *Fargesia* are the most beneficial and least invasive. Alternatively, you can use what the Chinese call the "cannon mouth". Lay some terracotta plant pots on their sides, fixed at an angle and with their mouths pointing at the problem, to bounce harmful chi back out of the garden (see below).

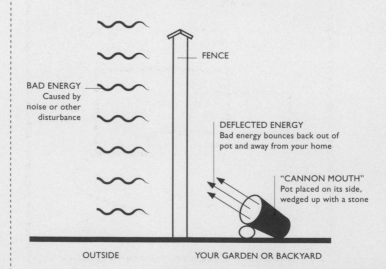

FENCE

BAD ENERGY
Caused by
noise or other
disturbance

DEFLECTED ENERGY
Bad energy bounces back out of
pot and away from your home

"CANNON MOUTH"
Pot placed on its side,
wedged up with a stone

OUTSIDE   YOUR GARDEN OR BACKYARD

If you want to be subtle about it, you can hide the pots with plants or a rockery. (An added benefit is that hedgehogs, which are traditionally seen as protective animals, like hiding in the pots.)

DOCTOR'S ORDERS

Problem: Your garden is overlooked by a "poison arrow".
Remedy: Plant hedges, bamboos or tall trees to screen you from the problem. At the edge of the garden you could add a hedge, or prickly plants such as holly, which act as "protector warriors". Another remedy is a wall or fence, but don't build it high or it can isolate your home from its surroundings.

Stirring the dragon's breath

Dragons, the most powerful and lucky animals in feng shui, symbolically live in rolling landscapes (see page 24). It's a good idea, therefore, to create different ground levels in your garden, like the rounded hills of the dragon's home, to stimulate the "dragon's breath" (*sheng chi*), or beneficial chi. Sunken areas, with seating and decorative plants, provide secluded, intimate spaces; they also, in effect, make fences higher and more protective. Examples of beneficial raised areas include rockeries for alpine plants, and herb gardens near kitchens.

Designs like these also fit the ancient Eastern principle that you should never be able to see a garden fully from one vantage point. Ideally, you should be able to journey through your garden, coming across areas with different atmospheres, and with lovely surprises such as sculptures, water features or flowering shrubs. Sunlight and shade can also help to create different moods and energies.

Balance and proportion

In a feng shui garden, "less is more" (*chiao te, chiao ta te*). The garden should feel spacious and not at all overcrowded. The plants and other features should be in proportion to each other, and nothing should dominate or overwhelm the space. Always leave the centre of your garden clear, with no large plants, ornaments or sheds.

Whatever you plant or put into the garden should look natural, as though it has been there for a long time. To create extra interest and promote good chi, you need to include a variety of textures, heights and shapes. In feng shui, it's also good practice to place key shrubs, bushes and trees asymmetrically.

Filling in missing areas

If your house has "missing areas" (see page 16) or is an "L" shape, you can correct the problem by "filling in" the areas, in a way that suits the pa kua location (see page 111), to include them in your garden.

One ideal way is to build a patio there, to give you an area for meals, activities and socializing. Patio doors are ideal for connecting the energy of your garden to that of your house. You can also use trees and lights. For example, you could install bright lights in a patio in the south to enhance the fire energy there, or plant fairly tall trees behind the house (see page 124) to protect the back of your property. To complete the missing area and give it life, add lighting at the corner.

Friendly gates

At the front of the house, wide, "friendly" gateways (*men kou*) are best. Ideally, you should have two gates, which open inward and are fairly low, to promote friendly, welcoming energy. The gates should be a suitable colour and material for the pa kua location (see page 111).

Meandering paths

The drive or path should curve toward the house, to provide gently moving chi; straight paths let the chi flow too fast. The most auspicious route is from east to west, to follow the sun. Ideal surfaces depend on the pa kua location. However, avoid crazy paving – it shatters the chi.

Cover the edges of a straight path or crazy paving with low-growing plants such as creeping thymes or camomile, to balance the energies. Alternatively, put plants, in rounded pots that suit the pa kua location (see page 111), on the edges of the path.

Water features

Ponds or fountains can provide strong, flowing chi as long as you locate them with care. Site ponds in dappled shade: avoid deep shade, which would make the water stagnant, or full sunlight, which would encourage weeds and algae. It's especially good if the feature is visible from the

Auspicious water features

Pebble ponds or very small fountains have the best feng shui, because they mimic natural springs. Big fountains, on the other hand, are seen as unnatural and thus undesirable.

If you want to keep fish, the most auspicious types are goldfish (traditionally called "baby dragons") or koi (which turn into "dragons"). It's best to have nine fish – eight gold and one black – or multiples of nine. In a very small water feature, you could have three fish: two gold and one black.

living room, dining room or conservatory, to enhance their pleasant energy. Don't have it facing a kitchen or bathroom, or near a compost heap or septic tank, because it can boost bad energy from those areas. If you can't move a water feature, hide the "bad" area with plants, a trellis or a rockery, as appropriate for the pa kua sector (see pages 112–13).

Fences and decking

Curved shapes are best for fences and decking. Vertical fencing symbolizes upward growth and is preferable to horizontal slats (which represent "strangle lines" constricting the chi).

These structures are usually wooden; if they're in a pa kua sector that doesn't suit wood, paint or stain the wood to the right colour. If you have a fence, paint it to suit most or all of the sectors it occupies.

Working with elemental energies

To produce the correct blend of energies, you need to choose plants, ornaments and structures that suit the pa kua locations and work well with each other. The diagram opposite shows the sectors and their ruling elements; areas of life that you can improve by working on each one; and examples of colours, materials and features that suit each one. See page 146 for a list of suggested plants for each sector.

Barbecues work well in fire, earth or wood sectors. However, their fire energy will clash with metal and water sectors. You should also keep "fiery" plants such as fuchsias out of these sectors.

Water features are best placed in the southeast, where they enhance "richness of life". The worst pa kua locations are south, northeast and southwest, because the energy in these sectors clashes with water. Wood suits most sectors, but avoid having wooden features such as decking in the southwest, where it will drain the earth energy there.

Earth symbols, such as large areas of stone, paving or gravel, work very well in earth and metal sectors, but try not to have them in the north (water), or the east or southeast (wood), because they will block the natural energies of those sectors.

The elements in your garden

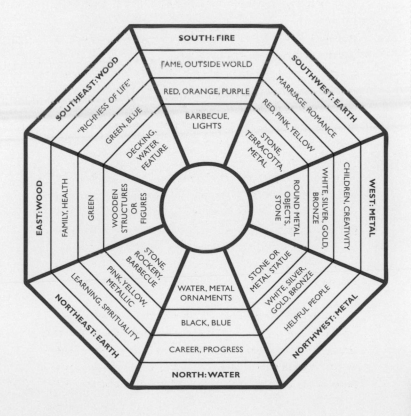

SOUTH: FIRE
FAME, OUTSIDE WORLD
RED, ORANGE, PURPLE
BARBECUE, LIGHTS

SOUTHEAST: WOOD
"RICHNESS OF LIFE"
GREEN, BLUE
DECKING, WATER FEATURE

SOUTHWEST: EARTH
MARRIAGE ROMANCE
RED, PINK, YELLOW
STONE, TERRACOTTA, METAL

EAST: WOOD
FAMILY, HEALTH
GREEN
WOODEN STRUCTURES OR FIGURES

WEST: METAL
CHILDREN, CREATIVITY
WHITE, SILVER, GOLD, BRONZE
ROUND METAL OBJECTS, STONE

NORTHEAST: EARTH
LEARNING, SPIRITUALITY
PINK, YELLOW, METALLIC
STONE, ROCKERY, BARBECUE

NORTHWEST: METAL
HELPFUL PEOPLE
WHITE SILVER, GOLD, BRONZE
STONE OR METAL STATUE

NORTH: WATER
CAREER, PROGRESS
BLACK, BLUE
WATER, METAL ORNAMENTS

曲
线
与
色
彩

Location, location, location

North: Greens or blues, dark blues or a little black (water), and whites, creams or greys (metal) work well here. A north garden is ideal for a water feature or a birdbath. A good ornament would be a tortoise (symbolic animal of the north) or a "protector-warrior" figure such as a samurai or Michelangelo's *David*. Make sure statues don't face a kitchen, bathroom or compost heap, because they can increase bad chi from those areas.

Northeast: The chi in the northeast supports spirituality, so this is a good site for a quiet area, or for martial arts, yoga or meditation. You can enhance the chi with lights, or a spiritual ornament such as a Buddha. A northeast garden is ruled by earth, so is ideal for terracotta pots, pebbles, gravel, rockeries or even stone buildings. Herbs and alpines work well here; choose oranges and reds (fire), or pinks and yellows (earth). Metallic colours, as in golden and silver thymes, also fit well.

East: The east supports family, health, long life and ambition. Boost the wood energy with lots of green, some yellows, reds and purples, and a little blue. Bamboo, pines and yellow chrysanthemums promote longevity, and ornamental fruit trees bring in beneficial chi. A garden in the east is ideal for decking, a trellis or a wooden sculpture (such as a crane or deer, symbols of longevity). You could also represent the dragon, symbolic animal of the east, with a small raised area or a dragon statue.

Southeast: The chi here promotes "richness of life". To enhance the wood energy, have lots of small, mainly evergreen shrubs, or a lawn. Greens, yellows and blues are excellent colours here. A water feature will bring good luck; fish ponds are particularly auspicious. Alternatively, you could just have a statue of a frog or a fish, or a collection of shells.

South: The south symbolizes sociability and communication, making it ideal for barbecues and parties. This sector should be well lit. Choose flowers and shrubs in bright reds, yellows, oranges and purples; fuchsias are excellent because they are fiery colours and look like little lanterns. Greens (wood) are also beneficial. This is a good site for decking, paving or gravel. An ideal decoration would be a statue of a phoenix, rooster, parrot or pheasant – or even some real birds, such as peacocks.

Southwest: The southwest, symbolizing relationships and couples, is ideal for a hidden garden. Good colours are pink or yellow (earth), or touches of orange, red or purple (fire); silver or gold is also beneficial, because it blends earth and metal. Earth and gravel, and stone, terracotta or metal ornaments, work well. Paired statues of lovers or birds are very good luck; traditional symbols are cranes, with one preening as the other stands guard, or mandarin ducks, believed to mate for life.

West: The west is the sector of children, new projects, problem-solving, pleasure, creativity and relaxation. Enhance its metal energy with whites, creams, greys, silvers and golds, and shiny, rounded metal ornaments. In addition, you can blend metal with earth symbols such as pink or yellow flowers, stones, or terracotta pots. The west is the realm of the white tiger, whose unpredictable power has to be controlled; plant fragrant white, cream, pink or lavender flowers, to "keep the tiger dozing".

Northwest: The northwest is the zone of helpful people, networking and removal of obstacles. The colours used in the west (see above) would also be beneficial here. You can enhance the chi of a garden here with stone, gravel, rounded cobblestones, and metal or stone sculptures, especially of "protector-warriors", as for the north (see above).

WORK SPACE
The dragon's lair

If you're laying out a distinct office space or just adapting part of a room, make it a real work space; don't be half-hearted. As the Chinese say, "When you sit . . . sit. When you stand . . . stand. Don't wobble!" Aim to make it different from the rest of the house or room so it won't look or feel like home. While you're working, let the work take over. Afterwards, shut the door or neaten the area and leave it behind.

Work spaces need yang chi – lively energy that will support you and give you extra determination and strength if your own energy starts to flag. You need to make the space work well for you.

The seat of power

Your desk should command the room. Ideally, it should be in a corner with solid walls behind it and a good view of the window and door. This site is traditionally called the "dragon's lair" (*lung shou hsueh*) or "where the tiger leaps, the dragon soars". It is also called the "boss's position".

This location forms a strong base. Its chi will boost decision-making, problem-solving, authority and determination. Try to avoid positions with no view of the door or window, or in which you have your back to doors, windows or long corridors; they can make you feel insecure and restless. These ideas developed centuries ago, when feng shui was used solely to benefit the rich and powerful in China. Such people applied them for protection against attack or assassination.

To make your seat even more secure, choose a chair with a high back. This type of chair is like a traditional Chinese gravestone: supportive and protective. Low seats, on the other hand, will weaken your energy.

A classic "dragon's lair"

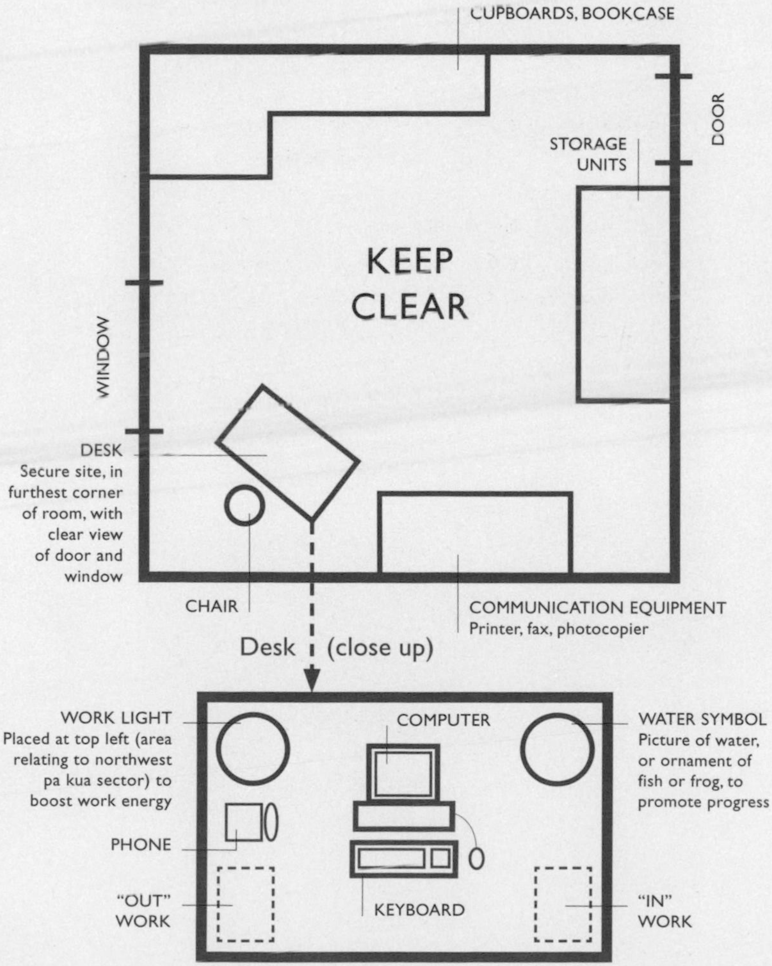

CUPBOARDS, BOOKCASE

DOOR

STORAGE
UNITS

KEEP
CLEAR

WINDOW

DESK
Secure site, in
furthest corner
of room, with
clear view
of door and
window

CHAIR

COMMUNICATION EQUIPMENT
Printer, fax, photocopier

Desk (close up)

WORK LIGHT
Placed at top left (area
relating to northwest
pa kua sector) to
boost work energy

COMPUTER

WATER SYMBOL
Picture of water,
or ornament of
fish or frog, to
promote progress

PHONE

"OUT"
WORK

KEYBOARD

"IN"
WORK

DOCTOR'S ORDERS

Problem: You have no choice but to sit with your back to a door or large window.

Remedy: Use a high-backed chair to protect your back. Vertical blinds can shield you from a window. (Never use Venetian blinds, because their horizontal lines "chop up" the chi.) In addition, place a small mirror, a picture with a reflective frame, or a shiny, rounded bowl or vase on the desk so you can see the window or door reflected in it.

Energizing your work area

Keep your desktop as clear as possible to let the chi flow freely. Have spaces for your in-tray and out-tray, and keep stationery stored away if you're not using it. Keep unused equipment in drawers or cupboards.

On the wall behind you, it can help to put up a small picture of a mountain such as Fuji Yama, Uluru (Ayers Rock) or Everest. It will protect you in the way that mountains protect a building (see page 124).

To encourage progress, you can put a small water symbol on the desk. It's traditional to have a carp figurine, but a fish-shaped ornament in shiny metal, a shell, or a picture of the sea or a waterfall will do just as well. To help you focus on work, have only one or two personal items.

It's also useful to put a lamp in the top left corner of the desk: this area relates to the northwest pa kua sector, which has to do with helpful people and removal of obstacles. It helps to turn on the lamp half an hour before starting work. This creates an energy-filled environment known as the "place of the shining mind" (*kuang hain fang chih*). Otherwise, turn it on as soon as you begin and turn it off when you stop.

Stimulating helpful chi

Keep the centre of the work area clear to encourage a gentle, curving flow of chi. Sharp corners on walls and furniture can help to boost the energy levels, but too many straight edges can cause stress, headaches, stiff necks, short tempers and eye pain. Soften these edges by using lights such as uplighters and desk lamps; rounded metal accessories if your office is in earth or metal locations; or broad-leaved plants in wood or fire sectors. If your office has any alcoves, which can trap stagnant chi, put a plant or computer there to stir the energy.

If your office is near or facing a bathroom, the draining effect of the "filthy" water can suck good chi out of your home. "Hide" the bathroom and block its energy by hanging a mirror on the outside of the door.

It's best to put bookshelves in a far corner of your work space. Don't have them too near a desk because they form "strangle lines" that splinter the chi. If you have to have bookshelves near a desk, place books vertically, and pull them forward so their spines overlap the edges of the shelves.

Effective lighting

Make sure you have enough natural and artificial light, which will help to stimulate the chi. For general light, uplighters are better than ceiling-mounted lights because they direct chi upward. You'll also need a lamp for your desk or bench and extra lights if you have a seating area for guests.

The power of computers

Computers generate good yang energy and can be especially beneficial in the east or northwest pa kua sectors. It helps to put an amethyst crystal on top of a computer monitor; the crystal will purify the chi and combat static electricity, which might otherwise cause you stress and bad headaches.

If you have extra communications equipment, such as a fax machine or a scanner, put it on a separate table against a solid wall. The best position is in the south pa kua sector, where the energy promotes communication and connections to the outside world.

Spaces for different activities

If you have a whole room as your work area, divide it into spaces for different functions. Choose one space for your main work site and perhaps another area for activities or communications. If your work includes receiving visitors or entertaining, you may need a third area.

If the room covers more than one pa kua sector, have your work area in the sector with the most active energy. If you regularly receive business visitors, put a low table and a couple of comfortable chairs in a sector where the energy is lower (for example, the southwest).

Arranging space for group events

Group events, such as meetings, are best held in a separate room or area rather than your office. Meeting rooms often occupy more than one pa kua location. The east/southeast/south is the best combination, because the energies in these pa kua sectors support wealth, strong relationships and sociability, but any group of sectors can be used.

In a formal meeting, the chairperson should sit furthest from the door, with solid walls behind him or her and a clear view of the door and windows. This seat, called the "honoured guest" position, provides protection and authority. For formal meetings, use a rectangular table, placed at a slight angle to guide the chi in a curving path. For informal meetings a round table is better, so everyone has equal importance.

Planning a meeting

If you're hosting a meeting that includes different activities, carry out each one in a different part of the room. In a space that occupies two or three pa kua sectors, you can make use of the energy in each area. In this example, the boardroom table is in the north, where the energy promotes career and progress. There is a presentation area in the northeast, the sector related to learning. The room also has an informal area in the east, where the chi supports ambition; the east is also associated with health, so would be good for a buffet table.

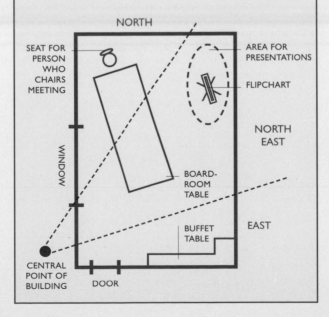

Colours to suit your job

When choosing your decor, have in mind the main activity you'll be doing in the room. Bright colours are more yang and will boost your energy, while dark or pastel colours are more yin, with a calming effect. It's best to stick to two or three plain colours, rather than patterns.

Yellow is good for almost any work space and pa kua location, because it stimulates the chi and promotes communication. If your job is particularly stressful, surround yourself with earthy colours such as terracotta, caramel or apricot, to calm and support you.

If your work space covers two or more pa kua sectors and your decor is wrong for one sector, cover the "wrong" colour or material with symbols of the correct element (see page 101).

Applying the pa kua to your work space

If your work space is within your home, it will be covered by your overall pa kua of the house. However, the ideal place for a work area is actually a free-standing shed or garage, which would have its own full pa kua, due to being a separate building.

Location, location, location

North: The chi in the north gives strong protection and encourages progress and ambition. Good colours are white, cream, grey, gold, silver and black. A wooden floor is ideal, as are chrome and stainless-steel furnishings. You can also use rich green colours and broad-leafed plants.

Northeast: The chi in the northeast aids quick thinking, decision-making and studying. Stimulate it with rich, earthy colours such as terracotta, yellow, lilac and caramel. Add the strong, lively metal energy of white, cream, grey, and chrome or stainless steel furniture.

East, southeast: These sectors are good for general administrative work. The east supports ambition, while the southeast represents prosperity and "richness of life". Good colours are greens (wood), yellows and touches of red or purple (fire). Wooden floors are ideal. Plants and small water features also stimulate helpful chi.

South: If you work in an area such as sales or the media, an office here is ideal for helping you to promote yourself. The south connects the home to the outside world; it also represents sociability, reputation and communication. Boost the ruling fire energy with bright lights, vibrant greens, yellows, reds and purples, and wooden floors or furniture.

Southwest: In this nurturing sector, the chi is really too sluggish for decision-making or setting targets. However, the southwest can be used for counselling, one-to-one therapies or human resources. In this case, enhance the sector's earth energy with rich, warm earth colours (see Northeast, above), and include some metallic colours and objects.

West: An office here is perfect for creativity, problem-solving, lateral thinking and new projects; in fact, both Charles Dickens and Rudyard Kipling had "writing rooms" in the west of their homes. Choose metal colours and objects, such as white, cream, grey, chrome, silver, gold and stainless steel. Add some rich earth colours for a stimulating blend.

Northwest: If you are a CEO, MD or high-level manager, this sector is ideal; it's traditionally seen as the boss's place. Don't let anyone else take it over. The most beneficial colour is silver-grey, which represents authority and decision-making. You can also add more metal (see West, above), and include earth symbols to form a rich blend of energies.

MODERN FENG SHUI FACTORS

Our busy 21st-century environment gives us many conveniences but it can also interfere with the natural flow of chi. The information in this section shows you how to use feng shui to help you make the most of the chi coming into your home from the surrounding areas, and how to protect yourself from disrupted energies. You'll also learn how you can give your home a burst of new energy.

从
坏
到
好

SOLVING LOCATION PROBLEMS
From bad to good

Just as people are affected by the energy of their homes, the buildings themselves are influenced by the overall balance of energies in the landscape. In the words of the traditional feng shui saying, "all is connected to all" (*ch'uan pu lien chieh*). A good location can enhance the natural flow of chi that you and your home absorb. On the other hand, places that are associated with speed and noise, or with pain, death, stagnation and dereliction, can have a harmful effect on you.

This chapter starts by showing sites with ideal feng shui. However, even if your home is not in an ideal site or if you have sources of negative energy in your surroundings, there's no need to worry; feng shui can help you to make the best of any location, no matter how challenging.

Ideal landscapes

The ancient masters of feng shui picked out certain features in landscapes that would support the people living there and enhance the "dragon's breath", or the ideal form of chi (see page 39). Two examples are rounded hills or mountains that wrap around a site to protect it, and waterfalls and streams, which represent progress, growth and travel. These ideas can easily be updated for the modern world.

In an ideal site, the "dragon" side (the left-hand side, as you look out from inside your front door) would be slightly higher than the "tiger" side (the right-hand side). The back of the home would be protected by hills, tall buildings or even tall trees, these features acting in the same way as the mountains in a Chinese landscape. A low wall or hedge at the front of the property would give further protection and support.

Good locations

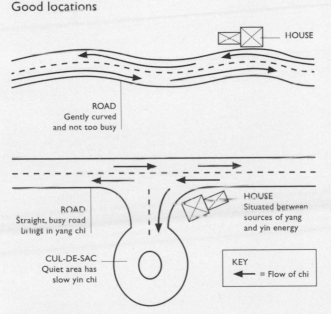

ROAD
Gently curved
and not too busy

ROAD
Straight, busy road
brings in yang chi

HOUSE

HOUSE
Situated between
sources of yang
and yin energy

CUL-DE-SAC
Quiet area has
slow yin chi

KEY
◄— = Flow of chi

Beneficial roads

Roads carry the same flowing energy as rivers. The best site for a home
is beside a two-way road that runs parallel to the front of the house.
The road should preferably be curving, and not too busy or too quiet,
so it produces a healthy flow of chi. Pedestrian crossings or traffic lights
that control the movement of traffic are also beneficial.

Another good position is a transitional point between a very yin
area and a very yang area, which has a blend of the two energies. One
example would be a house at the mouth of a cul-de-sac, because it sits
at the transitional point between the yin energy of the cul-de-sac and
the yang energy of the road outside.

从
坏
到
好

Rushing chi

Feng shui masters used to identify sites as "dangerous" if they were too close to water, almost surrounded by water or directly facing running water. In modern life, roads can present the same hazards. Fast, busy roads, overpasses and railroads speed up the energy around your home, making it too yang. They rush good chi past your property, instead of letting it enter. If you imagine that roads are rivers, busy, straight roads, or busy one-way streets can erode the energy of houses on either side, in the same way that fast-flowing rivers can erode riverbanks.

Poison arrows

"Poison arrows" are a form of bad chi that directly hit your house. The "arrows" come from sharp corners or edges, including roof apexes, wall corners, lamp posts, bus stops, T-junctions, electricity pylons (transmission masts), cellphone masts, power lines and electricity substations.

For example, a house at a T-junction is like one facing a fast river. Imagine the road as a river in flood, rushing at the house. The flow of chi is far too quick, and can cause stress, arguments and illness – in China and Japan, a house here is called a "house of the short-lived". You need to take specific steps to guard against poison arrows (see page 130).

Stagnant, toxic chi

Certain features in a landscape slow down the chi, making it too yin to be useful. The Chinese refer to this very stagnant, unmoving yin chi as "smelly" (fa ch'ou wei). The most obvious examples are bodies of stagnant water. Ancient sites, graveyards, battlefields and burial sites, being associated with death, also give off this energy. To understand the toxic effect, imagine water soaking through a graveyard, and compare it to pure, clean running water.

In modern towns or cities, places associated with death include doctors', dentists' or veterinary surgeons' premises, hospitals, and funeral homes. A very quiet road, or the end of a cul-de-sac, can trap stagnant energy, just like a sluggish river or a dank, smelly pond.

One unusual sign of stagnant yin chi in or around your home can be the presence of a wasps' nest. Wasps are often attracted to yin chi and may build nests near stagnant water or leaks. (Australian Aboriginal people actually watch wasps' behaviour to help them to find water.)

Bad locations for a house

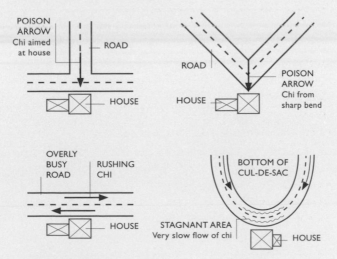

Electromagnetic energy

Feng shui teaches that everything is made up of vibrations. Certain types of vibration are apparent even in our everyday world. Sound is one type, comprising waves that move through air, water or solid substances.

Electromagnetic energy is another type. It occurs naturally as light (of which colours are different vibrations). It can also be generated by man-made objects, from cellphones to electricity substations.

We're surrounded by an electromagnetic "soup", which our bodies absorb. If the "soup" is made from healthy ingredients it will be good for us, but if it has poisoned or mutated ingredients it will harm our chi and take its toll on our systems. Some people are especially sensitive to this energy, but it can affect all of us.

In the landscape, electricity pylons (transmission masts), cellphone masts or electricity substations produce hot spots of twisting or spiralling energy, which can adversely affect the immune system. As a result, people can absorb "microwaved", scrambled chi. Some studies have even suggested that illnesses such as ME, multiple sclerosis and many types of cancer may be linked to this twisted energy.

Black streams

Scrambled electromagnetic energy can also be generated naturally underground, forming "black streams", or lines of geopathic stress. One source of black streams is water, such as streams and wells. The other, more powerful source is ley lines, which are lines of strong, moving electromagnetic energy. In ancient times, ley lines, or places where the lines crossed, were often used as sites of stone circles, witches' covens, and even churches and other holy places.

In my work I come across black streams in about 1 in 30 homes. They tend to occur in very flat, marshy areas, with lots of drainage ditches and pools – or in rugged, hilly or mountainous areas with hard rock, through which water flows. Sometimes, a black stream passing under a house "splits it in two", disrupting its chi. Often, the problem is made worse by nearby pylons, substations or cellphone masts.

Highly sensitive people

Certain people are more susceptible than others to black streams. Animals are also highly sensitive to them. For example, dogs have fairly yang energy and will avoid these places. However, cats have a more yin energy and may actually sleep on spots above black streams. Some people are sensitive to any source of electromagnetic energy, and the mixture of natural black streams and disrupted energy from man-made sources can be devastating to their energy levels.

Deflecting harmful energy

The answer for any of these environmental problems is usually the same. Protect yourself and your home by creating a screen or a good energy field between you and the source of the harmful chi (see below). The feng shui rule is: if you can see a problem it can affect you, but if you can screen or hide it, you help to take the effect away.

While you can often avoid sources of electromagnetic energy in your surroundings (or at least screen yourself from them), black streams are very hard to find and remedy. It may be best to seek help from a feng shui expert. I've discovered that the only way to find them is by dowsing, in which I use metal rods or crystals to detect the energy. It's possible to block energy from a black stream by using earth symbols, such as earthy colours, stone, tiles or crystal – but it's a tough job.

Stimulating good chi

If you have a garden, use it as a protective "moat". Walls or fences, hedges, trees or lines of bamboo are all good ways to hide a hazardous feature and stop harmful chi from entering (see also page 106).

Inside your home, use colours, light, plants and mirrors, depending on the pa kua sectors, to enhance the flow of beneficial chi. Suitable colours and materials for each section of the pa kua are given on pages 143–5. There are also various ways to protect particular rooms from harmful chi; for further details, see Section 2.

Guarding against poison arrows

Doors and windows allow chi into your home, so you need to check each one for poison arrows. At windows, vertical blinds can help to disperse harmful chi. Plants or rounded metal ornaments, depending on the pa kua location, can also be highly effective at a window. Clear quartz crystals are a traditional remedy; if they're not to your taste, you can benefit just as much from using a crystal ornament or bowl.

Alternatively, you could put protective figures on window sills, facing the poison arrows. Dogs are ideal guardians, so if you have a dog, a picture of him or her would work well here. Other good protectors are fierce animals such as lions, cheetahs or bears. However, don't use a tiger, because its energy is too strong for houses (see pages 24–5).

The Chinese traditionally use "protector-warrior" (*chan shih*) figures such as Kuan Kong (god of wealth and protection). A modern equivalent might be a picture of a leader you admire or a model of a character such as Superman. One fan of the British TV show *Doctor Who* used a dalek; this scary alien might not appeal to everyone, but it worked for him.

Identifying problems around your home

We know how a physical irritation, such as a drip in our sink, loud music or a repetitive car alarm, can wear us down. In the same way, a leaky or loud energy system around us will gradually damage our own chi. You need to apply the ABC of feng shui: Awareness, Balance, Control (see page 40). If you have a problem, you first need to find out what may be causing it, then balance the energies and bring it under control.

If you're buying a new home, try to avoid as many problem features as you can. Whenever I perform a consultation, I check maps before visiting the site, and while I'm there I walk around the area and ask the residents about good and bad features. A good test is to look from each window and note what you see. Anything you can see will affect you. If you're having problems in your present home, use the questions below to identify them, then look at the tips in this chapter and the relevant chapter in Section 2 to correct them.

Have you noticed a problem?

Ask yourself the following questions to find out if you have any of the problems covered in this chapter.

- Does the atmosphere in your home, or in a certain room, make you feel uncomfortable?
- Have you developed any health problems since you moved into your present home?
- If you have a health problem, do you feel better when you're away from home for some time?
- Can you see any "poison arrows" from doors or windows?
- Do you have any sources of toxic yin chi, such as a cul-de-sac or a graveyard, near your house?
- Do you have any pylons, cellphone masts or other sources of electricity near your house?
- Have any roads, drainage or sewage systems, phone masts or electrical systems been built near you in recent years?
- Have you experienced any problems in your health or life following the addition of these new features?

清新

SELLING OR REVITALIZING YOUR HOME
Refreshment

This chapter features simple, practical tips to help you to refresh the energies in your home. They're most useful if you're selling your home, because they'll allow new energy in and encourage you to move on. Some can be used when you first put your home up for sale, while others provide an instant lift when prospective buyers are about to call.

You can also apply these remedies if you've made a major change to your home, such as building an extension or changing the use of a room; they'll enable you to make the most of the new energy.

Finally, these tips can help you to prepare for life changes, such as marriage, a new baby or a new job, or before a big family celebration; you can use them to adjust the chi in your home simply to boost your own energy levels. Alternatively, they can ease you through a personal or family crisis, or just through a long, dark winter.

Preparing to sell your home

If you're selling your house, you need to prepare to move on and let someone else's new energy into the property. The tips given below will help you to make the break in your own mind. They will also make the house more welcoming for prospective buyers.

• Start packing away your possessions. If possible, keep the packed boxes and cases in one room, and cover them with protective sheets. This will show prospective buyers that you are serious about moving and that, symbolically, you're already on your way.

- Put away any family pictures, or personal ornaments such as soft toys, before anyone views the house. This action begins to empty the rooms of your personality, making the house feel less like your home. The rooms and other spaces will then be like a blank canvas, which will enable the prospective buyers to imagine themselves decorating and living in the house.

- Turn on all the lights in the house two to three hours before anyone comes to view it, to move and stimulate the chi. It's especially important to switch lights on in rooms that are seldom or never used, such as spare bedrooms or grown-up children's old rooms.

- Let lots of natural light into the landing and hallway, or turn on the lights and keep them brightly lit while people are looking around.

- Brighten up the living room with lots of light, and by adding touches of stronger, brighter "yang" colours in furnishings and accessories, as well as a vase or two of fresh flowers.

- In the bedrooms, make sure all the beds are freshly made. Have matching tables and lamps on both sides of double beds to promote harmonious energies.

- Cleaning up and neatening rooms before viewers arrive will help to freshen the chi. In addition, keep the doors of all rooms shut, so that the rooms hold on to their particular energy.

- Bring viewers into the kitchen first of all, because this is the "engine room" of the house, and work outward from there.

清
新

Blending yin and yang chi

To achieve the correct blend of energies for your lifestyle, you first need to set your intentions for your property as a whole. Try to decide whether you want a quiet retreat (more yin) or a busy space (more yang). A more yin atmosphere can be calming if you have a stressful work or family life, or to nurture young children or elderly people; a more yang feel may help if you work from home. Country homes are more yin, while city apartments tend to be more yang. You also need to balance the energy of your house with yin and yang features in the landscape, such as quiet churches or busy roads (see Chapter 12).

Use the questions below to help you to determine the right blend of yin and yang for you. Once you've done this, look at the balance of chi in each room (see Section 2).

ADD MORE YANG

• Do you work from home?

• Do you like socializing at home?

• Are you trying to get a promotion or new job?

• Are you feeling less confident or more depressed than usual?

• Are you about to begin a busy phase of your life, such as getting married, starting a new job or having a baby?

ADD MORE YIN

• Do you need to reduce the stress in your life?

• Do you have young children or elderly people living with you?

• Is your job busy or hectic and do you need a sanctuary?

• Are you about to retire and take life more gently?

• Do you have major health or emotional concerns, such as heart problems, high blood pressure or difficulty controlling anger?

Refreshing your house as a whole

The following guidelines will help to stimulate the "dragon's breath", or the ideal blend of chi (see page 39) throughout your home. They will also enable you to control clutter, which can be a major source of energy blockages. Whether you plan to change your decor or leave things as they are, these steps will freshen the feel of your home.

- Put your lights on for a few hours each day for five days. Turn on the lights by your front door, both inside and outside, from dusk until bedtime. During this time, these "welcoming lights" will raise the energy levels around the front door and hallway. In addition, turn on the landing lights upstairs to lift the chi on the upper floor and prevent it from flowing down the staircase.

- Generally, keep all internal doors closed, including sliding doors. By keeping each room shut, you allow it to build up its own blend of energies; the rooms should feel different as you pass from one to the next. They should then work more effectively to influence your life.

 • Once a week, open all doors and a few windows (except bathroom or toilet doors) to blow energy through the house. It is best to do this in the morning, when the flow of chi is very yang and active. Afterwards, keep the doors closed as usual (see above) to enable the refreshed energies to rebuild.

- Have a clearly defined purpose for each space in your home, including extensions, loft spaces and garages. Keep each room neat and have only the things you need in that room; these measures will help to prevent junk from collecting there.

清新

- If you have a spare room, give it a specific function, such as an ironing or dressing area, or a storage room. Whatever you use the room for, keep it neat to guarantee a free flow of chi.

- Any empty rooms within your home will be holding stale yin energy. To raise the energy levels, go into these rooms each day. Light and sound will also help to keep the chi moving; have the lights on for two or three hours a day (or, if possible, install a timer), and turn on the radio or play music for a while.

- If your children have left home, or if you have guest bedrooms, go into the unused rooms each day to maintain the level of chi and stop them from developing a still, museum-like yin energy. You could use the room for sitting and reading, or relaxing; in this way, you bring your energy into the space. Switch on the lights and use sound or music to lift the chi (see above).

- Unused objects or collections of junk can block the flow of chi around rooms. Every so often, go through each room and clear out the clutter. Get rid of anything you no longer use, need or like; throw it away, auction it off or give it to charity.

- If you wish to store unused items, put them all into one room and cover them with sheets or throws of appropriate colours for that pa kua location (see pages 143–5). If possible, stack the items together and put one sheet over everything. You'll then have one lump, causing one "blockage", rather than lots of blockages. If you need to store certain things permanently, rent a storage facility and get the "blockage" out of the house.

Refreshing specific areas

These tips will help you to enhance the chi in particular areas. Full information for each room is given in Section 2, and details about the pa kua locations are given in the Guide to the Pa Kua (see pages 140–7), but you can use the list below for instant reference.

- On the left-hand side of the main door as you look at it from the inside, hang a symbol of "flowing, good water", such as a small, metal-framed mirror or a small picture of a waterfall. This type of symbol is auspicious because it represents progress, movement and energy. If you have a water image here already, buy a new symbol to replace the old one.

- In bathrooms, take out all water symbols. Remove plants (which symbolize wood) because they worsen the draining water energy. Add earth colours, such as yellow, and symbols such as pebbles, to control the water. Keep the door closed and the toilet lid down.

- Place small amethyst crystals on top of electrical items such as TVs, computers, electricity meters and fuse boxes. The amethyst helps to cleanse the chi and combat the draining effect of static electricity.

- Place yellow flowers in your living room, hall and dining room; you can use either fresh ones or silk ones. They will stimulate the chi, encouraging communication and mental activity.

- In the north of your home, boost the water energy of this sector with blacks and blues, and perhaps a small water symbol such as a conch shell. You can also enhance the chi with large, broad-leaved

清
新

evergreen plants, whose wood energy will support water (see Constructive Cycle, page 35). Alternatively, you can add some metal symbols, such as whites and creams for walls or furnishings, or shiny metal ornaments.

- In the northeast of your home, especially if this is your living room, dining room or study, use metal uplighters to boost the lively energy there. The northeast is also excellent for electrical items such as a TV or music system. If you wish, you can enhance the spiritual energies with a Buddha, and with rounded clear quartz crystals.

- Enliven the east of your home with bamboo or other plants, and with flowers, all of which strengthen this sector's ruling wood energy. (However, don't use plants in bedrooms; their energy is too strong.) Rounded shapes, such as a green or jade egg ornament, are ideal in the living room.

- For a living room, dining room, study or extension in the southeast, the following steps can boost the chi for prosperity, health and strong relationships. Add water symbols, such as a fish tank, a picture of a lake or ocean, or a fish, shell or frog ornament. You can also include a *Crassula* (Chinese money plant) or a *Philodendron*. However, don't use any of these symbols in bedrooms, bathrooms or kitchens, because they clash with the energies of those rooms.

- If you have a living room, office or hallway in the south, boost the sector's fire energy with warm desert colours, such as reds, yellows and purples. Red or yellow flowers are excellent for raising energy. Large, broad-leaved plants (see north, above) are also good. If you need to enhance your connections with the outside world, add a picture or ornament of an exotic, brightly coloured bird, such as a pheasant, cockerel, peacock or phoenix.

- In the south and southwest, especially in living rooms and dining rooms, put down square or rectangular rugs in yellow or fiery colours. The angular shapes enhance yang chi, and the colours harmonize the elements of these sectors (fire and earth, respectively).

- Enrich the southwest of your home with earthy colours, such as terracotta, yellow, brown, caramel, lilac and lavender. These colours add to the friendly, "cuddly" energy of this sector and bring a deep harmony and stability to the home. However, you need to remove wood symbols such as plants, green colours and wooden flooring or furniture, and water symbols, because their energies disturb the chi in the southwest.

- In the west, bring in lots of metal colours and symbols, such as white, creams, greys and metal ornaments. These symbols will promote strength, determination and new opportunities.

- To boost the chi in the northwest, add shiny, rounded metal ornaments. They will have a stimulating, refreshing effect and dispel old, stagnant energy, making the chi flow more quickly.

- In the west and northwest, shiny, decorative metal bowls and vases can strongly enliven the chi. Brass, copper, stainless steel and chrome are excellent. Keep the bowls empty, because empty bowls are more powerful; they attract new energy.

GUIDE TO USING THE PA KUA

Advice on working with the energies of pa kua sectors

The sectors of the pa kua

The diagram below shows the pa kua. It gives the name of each sector, then, working inward, shows the areas of life that the sector supports, the associated colour(s) and element, and the symbolic trigram (and its name) for the sector. The pa kua is always used with north at the bottom and south at the top. The centre, or *tai chi,* is always left empty.

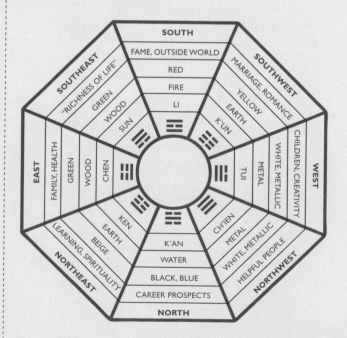

Relating the pa kua to your goals

You can use the energies of the pa kua sectors to support you in various aspects of your life. The list below gives the main areas of life that each sector can improve or revitalize for you. The box on page 142 shows how you can combine the powers of different sectors to help you to achieve particular goals.

NORTH • *Element: water* • *Represents: steady progress, movement – especially in career* • Work on the north if you are looking for promotion, a pay increase, more interesting work or a change of job or career.

NORTHEAST • *Element: earth* • *Represents: spirituality, learning, study, ancient wisdom* • The chi in the northeast is powerful and vibrant, so this sector is ideal for learning a foreign language, research or studying. It also boosts physical or spiritual energy, so is good for yoga, t'ai chi, meditation and martial arts, and supports complementary medicine, such as acupuncture, reiki or aromatherapy.

EAST • *Element: wood* • *Represents: ambition, growth, health, longevity, family well-being* • Try enhancing this sector if you wish to progress in your career or improve health or family relationships.

SOUTHEAST • *Element: wood* • *Represents: "richness" of life – prosperity, quality of life, strong relationships* • Try working with the chi in the southeast if you want to grow as a person and attract more of the "good things" in life.

SOUTH • *Element: fire* • *Represents: connections to the outside world* • Traditionally called the "bright hall" (*ming tang*), the south represents reputation, enthusiasm and strong, vibrant, "talkative" energy. If you work in sales, PR, advertising, show business or the media, or want to break into these careers, you should boost this sector. The chi here also supports popularity and sociability in general.

SOUTHWEST • *Element: earth* • *Represents: stability, intimate relationships, relaxation.* • This sector is ideal for a couple; it offers a relaxing retreat and can be used to nurture relationships. If you are a therapist seeing clients on a one-to-one basis, a room here can provide nurturing energy to help with emotional trauma.

WEST • *Element: metal* • *Represents: creativity, problem-solving, children's energy* • Try enhancing the west to boost lateral thinking, original ideas and creativity, especially in the arts. The west is also great for new beginnings. The chi supports children's energy, so it might help to work on the west if you want a baby.

NORTHWEST • *Element: metal* • *Represents: removal of obstacles, helpful people, important meetings, making decisions* • Enhancing the northwest will help you with most goals. The chi supports decisiveness, determination and authority. The sector should always be controlled by the householder or boss; if it's occupied by children or guests, those people may take over.

YOUR GOALS AND THE PA KUA

GOAL IN LIFE	SECTOR
Improving health	E, S, W, NW
Increasing confidence	S, W, N, NW
Relieving depression	W, S, E, N, NW, NE
Making a new start	W, NW, S, E, N, NE
Learning and research	NE, E, S, W, NW
Boosting career; promotion	NW, N, E, SE, S, W
Finding love; relationships	S, SW, W, NW
Boosting fertility	W, SW, S, NW, E
Improving communications	S, W, NW, W, SE

Enhancing each pa kua location

The suggestions given here will help you to create a rich blend of energies in each pa kua location, irrespective of which room it occupies. For details on boosting the energies in specific rooms, see the end of each chapter in Section 2.

NORTH

Colours: Green (wood); blue, shiny black (water); white, cream, silver (metal).

Materials: All metals, especially shiny ones such as stainless steel and chrome.

Ornaments: Tortoise (symbolic animal of north). Water symbols, such as water features, pictures of water, shells, ornaments of animals such as fish, frogs, toads. Rounded metal items such as vases. Also good for large, broad-leaved evergreen plants, such as rubber plant, Swiss cheese plant, *Crassula* (Chinese money plant).

Avoid: Earthy colours such as terracotta, caramel, peach, apricot; fiery colours such as reds, purples, yellows.

NORTHEAST

Colours: Terracotta, caramel, lilac, peach, toffee, oatmeal, matt black (earth); white, cream, grey, metallic colours; touches of yellows, reds, purples (fire).

Materials: Stone, metals.

Ornaments: Ancient or spiritual objects, such as pictures of old or holy buildings, mountains, Buddha, angels or gurus. Also crystals, especially clear quartz.

Avoid: Plants, green colours (wood); blues, water, water symbols.

EAST

Colours: Green (wood); blue, turquoise (water); yellows, reds, purples (fire).

Materials: Wood.

Ornaments: Large evergreen plants; water features and water symbols. Also pictures of family, older relatives and any ancestors, to boost family relationships.

Avoid: Whites, creams, greys, metal objects; terracotta, brown, caramel (earth).

Traditional lore

The east is the location of the dragon, so is an ideal place for a dragon ornament. The perfect location, in a home or a garden, is facing west, with a view of water. Never place the dragon above eye level when you are standing – this position is said to be too powerful. Don't position him facing a kitchen, bathroom or front door. Kitchen or bathroom views are disrespectful, while if you point the dragon toward the front door, you're symbolically asking him and his good luck to leave!

SOUTHEAST

Colours: As for east (see page 143); the two sectors work together. Green (wood); blue, turquoise (water); yellows, reds, purples (fire).

Materials: Wood.

Ornaments: Large evergreen plants; pictures of flowers or landscapes; water feature or aquarium, and water symbols. Also family pictures, pictures of older relatives and any ancestors, to boost family relationships.

Avoid: Whites, creams, greys, metal colours; terracotta, brown, caramel (earth).

SOUTH

Colours: Reds, purples, yellows (fire). Also greens (wood), terracotta, browns, peach, lavender (earth).

Materials: Fire (as in fireplaces and barbecues).

Ornaments: Bright lights; bright flowers, such as poppies and sunflowers; pictures or ornaments of exotic birds, such as phoenix, parrot, pheasant or rooster, or of galloping horses. Large evergreen plants. To enhance communication and fame, use posters of favourite films or film stars, with happy, positive themes.

Avoid: Blue, water symbols, metals or metallic colours.

SOUTHWEST

Colours: Earth colours, especially rich terracottas, matt black and stone/oatmeal. Some white, cream, grey, metallic colours; touches of yellows, reds, purples (fire).

Materials: Stone, some metal.

Ornaments: To enhance love and romance, use pictures of yourself and your partner (with no one else), or other loving couples by themselves. Alternatively, use pairs of ornaments, such as candles, rose quartz crystals, lights or lamps. Can also use symbols of earth, love and passion.

Avoid: Plants, greens, blues, water.

WEST

Colours: Metal colours, such as white, cream, grey; earth colours, such as yellow, terracotta, peach, apricot.

Materials: Shiny metals; copper and brass, traditionally called "transformers of energy", are said to be especially powerful in the west and northwest.

Ornaments: Rounded metal objects, such as bells, bowls, vases; empty bowls represent spaces waiting to be filled and contain especially powerful energy. Symbols of fun, creativity and lateral thinking, such as music, books, surrealist or abstract art, funny pictures. You could also have a little picture or ornament symbolizing water. To boost fertility, use empty bowls, or pictures of babies or children.

Avoid: Plants (wood); fire colours or symbols.

NORTHWEST

Colours: Metal colours, such as white, cream and especially silver-grey; some earth colours, such as terracotta, peach, apricot, yellow.

Materials: Metal; stone, marble and granite are also particularly good.

Ornaments: Symbols of powerful, helpful figures, such as ornaments of elephants, images of admired leaders, or images of spiritual beings such as angels.

Avoid: Plants (wood); fire colours or symbols.

Garden plants for each pa kua sector

The suggestions given below include plants that will enhance each pa kua sector of a garden, as well as colours and plants that it's best to avoid. It's a good idea to repeat planting from one area in another suitable sector, so that the energies are "echoed" in the different areas.

NORTH

Plants: Small clumps of trees, *Eucalyptus*, Dragon Grass (*Ophiopogon planiscapus* 'Nigrescens'), *Hebe*, *Euonymus* 'Silver Queen', silver and golden thymes, gentians, *Senecio*, white clematis, *Ceanothus*.
Avoid: Fiery colours; earthy colours.

NORTHEAST

Plants: Alpines, herbs, silver and golden thymes, lavenders, cotton lavenders, *Choisya ternata* 'Sundance', curry plant, *Euphorbia* 'Fireglow', fuchsias, small red and golden acers (Japanese maples).
Avoid: Water, blues; too much green, especially evergreen.

EAST

Plants: Bamboos, for example: *Fargesia*, *Phyllostachys*; evergreens, dwarf conifers, such as *Pinus mugo* 'Mops', *Cupressus macrocarpa* 'Goldcrest'; lilacs, hydrangea; crab apple, cherry; chrysanthemums, fuchsias, narcissus, sunflowers, poppies.
Avoid: Metals, whites, creams, greys; earth colours.

SOUTHEAST

Plants: As for the east, with a few more blues, such as *Festuca glauca* 'Bluegrass', *Ceanothus*. *Eucalyptus*, juniper 'Blue Star'. Also evergreens such as *Hebe*, green box, laurel and dwarf conifers such as *Pinus mugo* 'Mops'.
Avoid: Metals, whites, creams, greys; earth colours.

SOUTH

Plants: Evergreens, red acers (Japanese maples), azalea, rhododendron, red camellia, red magnolia, *Pieris*, poppies, fuchsias, *Euphorbia* 'Fireglow', sage, coriander, aquilegia, sunflower, Red Hot Poker, narcissus, pansies, geraniums.

Avoid: Blues (water); whites, creams, greys (metal).

Traditional lore

In China and Japan, it was traditional to have pear trees outside theatres, and actors were often called "Children of the Pear Tree". If you want to break into showbusiness or the media, it can help to plant a pear tree (*Pyrus*) in the south, the sector relating to fame and reputation.

SOUTHWEST

Plants: Red or yellow acers (Japanese maples), red peony, also *Artemisia*, lavender, *Senecio*, cotton lavender, curry plant, *Choisya ternata* 'Sundance'.

Avoid: Lots of green (wood); water, blues.

WEST

Plants: Metallic colours, such as *Carex comans* 'Bronze', *Pittosporum* 'Tobira'. Fragrant lavenders, cotton lavenders, honeysuckles, sweet peas, curry plants, *Choisya ternata* 'Sundance', white camellias, white, yellow or pink azaleas, *Viburnum*.

Avoid: Fiery reds and purples; too much green.

NORTHWEST

Plants: Whites, creams, greys; metallic colours, eg *Carex comans* 'Bronze', *Pittosporum* 'Tobira'.

Avoid: Lots of greens or evergreens (wood); fiery reds and purples.

GLOSSARY

Ba gua   Alternative English spelling of *pa kua*.

Chan shih   "Protector-warrior"; any item used to give strong protection.

Chi   The natural energy that flows around and within everything in the universe. Everything gives out chi, and everything absorbs chi.

Chia   A good, homely feeling.

Chiao ssu   "Strangle lines". Horizontal lines, such as bookshelf edges, Venetian blinds or washing lines, that disrupt and chop up the chi.

Chiao te, chiao ta te   The principle "less is more". Never overfill a space, or overdo feng shui remedies.

Ch'ao ... jih lo   "The snake's nest, the sun's rest"; a traditional Chinese term for a bedroom.

Ch'i ma yeh chi   "Riding the phoenix"; creating a balance of energies giving rise to success and perfection. Can also mean working on the south sector of the *pa kua* – location of the *phoenix*.

Chuang ho hsing yun "Loaded with luck". In feng shui, the ideal state for a building. Often symbolized by a well-placed, well-set dining table.

Compass School   An ancient form of feng shui, based on working with the chi in the eight main compass locations. It involves the use of a compass (or a special compass called a *lo pan*) to identify the sectors of the *pa kua*.

Constructive Cycle   A form of helpful interaction between the Five Elements, in which each supports the ones next to it. This cycle is used to boost certain elemental energies. The elements in the cycle are known as "friendly elements" (*yu shan te yao su*).

Dao/Daoism See *Tao/Taoism*.

Destructive Cycle Challenging interaction between the *Five Elements*, in which each one attacks certain others. In feng shui, you need to prevent clashes between elements. However, you can also use the Destructive Cycle to block harmful energy.

Dragon Celestial animal of the east, whose symbolic colours are green or azure and whose element is wood. The dragon embodies *yang* qualities: good energy, great luck and transformations of energy. It is said to live in rolling, hilly landscapes, and is associated with the left-hand side of a garden or building.

Dragon's breath (sheng chi) The ideal blend of *yin* and *yang* chi, which moves in a curving, "measured and meandering" way to enrich an area.

Eight Locations The eight sectors around the edge of the *pa kua*. Each is associated with a compass point: north, northeast, and so on. Each contains its own blend of *chi*.

Fa ch'ou wei "Smelly": an expression used for very stagnant *yin chi*.

Feng shui The use of light, colour and objects to enhance *chi* in an area. Many of the symbols and practices used in feng shui first appeared many centuries ago in China. The principle of blending different forms of energy originated in *Taoism*.

Five Elements Metal, earth, fire, water, wood. Also called *wu h'sing*, "the five things that are being done". The elements can interact with each other in either beneficial or controlling ways; see *Constructive Cycle* and *Destructive Cycle*. Each sector of the *pa kua* is ruled by a particular element.

Form School An ancient form of feng shui that is based on analyzing features in the landscape and working with their energies.

Fu "Meat cleaver": the term for an "L" shaped building, which has missing areas and sometimes a *tai chi* (central point) outside the walls.

Ho sheng "Good, flowing"; a term used to describe ideal *chi*.

Hsi mieh "Puts out the fire". A term used of a remedy that controls overly fierce energy; in particular, the use of water symbols to control fire energy.

Hsiao hua jun i te "Easy digesting"; the feng shui expression for a perfect blend of *chi* in a dining area.

Hsin tsang "Heart of the house"; a Chinese term for a dining room.

Hu kung chi "Tiger attacks"; a term for the trouble you may face if you provoke the energy of the *tiger*.

Jen t'zu The reassuring *chi* of the northwest *pa kua* sector – said to be like a "friendly, wise old father".

K'u te ching cheng "Bitter rivals, angry neighbours": items with clashing elemental energies (see *Destructive Cycle*) next to or opposite each other, such as an oven (fire) next to a sink (water) in a kitchen.

K'ung te "Empty" or "unused"; a term for a "missing" area on a floor plan (see page 17).

Kou chou "Drain". Describes the way in which *chi* can be drained from the home and lost through bathtub and basin plugholes and down toilets.

Kou "Mouth"; the traditional name for a main door into a property, which symbolically feeds the building.

Kuan ch'a chi fu "Observe and apply"; this is one of the original principles underlying feng shui.

Kuang hain fang chih "Place of the shining mind"; an ideal work space or study area.

Lien chin shu "Alchemy". A very old term for the practice of feng shui. It refers to the blending of *chi*.

Ling hsiu A traditional name for the northwest sector of the *pa kua*. The name means "boss's location" or "area of authority".

Liu tung "Constantly flowing": a term used to describe healthy *chi*.

Lo pan A special type of compass used by feng shui practitioners in the *Compass School* to identify the sectors of the *pa kua*.

Lo shu See *magic square*.

Magic square The name for the set of numbers from 1 to 9 that is associated with each sector of the *pa kua*. Each number relates to the elemental energy of that pa kua sector. The numbers are also associated with *yin* and *yang* energy.

Ma pei "On the horse's back". A term used for a colour appropriate for a certain *pa kua* sector, which is laid on top of a "wrong" colour to balance the energies. Whichever colour sits on top, or "rides the horse", overcomes the energy of the one underneath.

Measured and meandering The ideal way for *chi* to flow: in a curving path, and not too fast or too slowly.

Men kou A term used to denote friendly, welcoming gateways.

Neng li shih li "Strong energy and power"; a perfect cocktail of *chi*.

Pa kua An eight-sided diagram (the name means "eight-sided shape") that shows the *Eight Locations* and the *tui chi*. It includes the *trigrams*, elements, colours, *magic square* numbers and aspects of life relating to each sector. You overlay the pa kua on a floor plan so you can identify and work with the energies in a particular space.

Pei pu shan te "Doubling the badness": the harmful effect if a mirror reflects something inauspicious, such as a bathroom. See also *pu shan te*.

Peng tai "Bandage"; a term for an object that is placed over another one to correct the *chi* in a *pa kua* sector. One example might be a mirror hung over a fireplace to control the fire energy. Another way of "applying the bandage" is to lay a correct colour on top of a wrong one; see *ma pei*.

Phoenix Celestial animal of the south, whose symbolic colour is red and whose element is fire. The phoenix embodies the perfect combination of *yin* and *yang* energy, and represents success, enthusiasm for life and strong spirit. Phoenix energy can also be symbolized by a pheasant, peacock, rooster or sparrow.

Pi shou "Dagger". Usually used to describe a spiral staircase that "stabs" the heart of a building.

Poison arrows Straight lines, edges or corners that aim excessively *yang* energy (see *sha chi*) at you or your home, damaging your energy. They include sharp points on furniture or roofs of houses, and T-junctions.

Pu "Simplicity". A fundamental principle of *Taoism*, and an essential aim in feng shui.

Pu shan te "Badness". The term refers to the pollution or draining away of good *chi* and is particularly associated with bathrooms.

Sha chi Excessively *yang chi*, which rushes through or past a house and carries good energy away.

Sheng chi See *dragon's breath*.

Sheng ming ts'ai fu "Richness of life": not only wealth, but also good quality of living and strong relationships.

Shih jui li See *poison arrows*.

Tai chi The centre of the *pa kua*; also called the "earthpot"; the point where different *chi* energies blend. It must be kept open and clear at all times.

Tao In *Taoism*, the universe and the connections between everything in it, including us.

Taoism A traditional Chinese system of philosophy based on people's relationships with the natural world. In feng shui, the Taoist masters developed the idea of blending natural energies.

Tao p'ien "Slicing blades": the term for closets or shelves placed above a bed or seat, which interfere with the energy of anyone lying or sitting underneath them.

Tiger Celestial animal of the west, whose symbolic colour is white and whose element is metal. The tiger embodies *yin chi* that is creative but unpredictable.

Tortoise Celestial animal of the north, whose symbolic colour is black and whose element is water. Known as the "protective warrior of the north", it symbolizes progress and protection.

Trigram A set of three lines that denote one of the *Eight Locations* on the *pa kua*. The lines represent a blend of *yin* and *yang* energies; yin is shown by a broken line and yang is indicated by a solid line.

Ts'ai fu See *sheng ming ts'ai fu*.

Tung te "Changing and moving": a term used to describe healthy *chi*.

Wing cheh See *Compass school*.

Wu A term for a state of creative, fertile emptiness; one of the ultimate aims in *Taoism*. *Wu* also refers to an opportunity waiting to happen. In feng shui, *wu* is associated with space and with empty containers – particularly metal bowls or vases placed in the west or northwest sectors of the *pa kua*.

Wu h'sing See *Five Elements*.

Yang The name for strong, active, positive, lively *chi*.

Yao sai ch'iang pi "Fortress walls"; structures or objects that are used to mark out particular areas and preserve their energies.

Yin The name for passive, stable, steady, slow *chi*.

Yu shan te yao su Friendly elements (see *Five Elements*), which can be used together to enhance helpful chi; see *Constructive Cycle*.

USEFUL WEBSITES

The websites listed here will tell you more about the author and feng shui, and show you where to buy home and garden items that fit in with feng shui principles.

www.fengshuidoctor.co.uk
Paul Darby's website has information on feng shui, details of consultations and other services offered by the author, and an on-line feng shui shop. Tel: 00 44 (0)1623 658390; e-mail: pauldarby@fengshuidoctor.co.uk

www.wofs.com
This site, run by international expert Lillian Too, has information on every aspect of feng shui, as well as articles by various other feng shui experts.

www.susanlevitt.com
Susan Levitt, a California-based feng shui practitioner, astrologer and tarot card reader, offers extra information and articles on feng shui.

www.hccollege.co.uk
The Horticultural Correspondence College runs gardening correspondence courses of all types. Paul has written a course for the college on designing a Japanese garden. Tel: 00 44 (0)1225 816700 or 0800 816700 (UK only); e-mail: info@hccollege.co uk

www.greenhillsgardencentre.co.uk
A great garden centre. Paul Lathrope, the owner, gives valuable advice and writes articles for various British magazines. Tel: 00 44 (0)1623 554418.

www.sittingspiritually.co.uk
This company makes sturdy wooden garden furniture, which is built to feng shui principles.

www.sallyannsheridan.com
Sallyann will give you wise advice on organizing your life. She also teaches workshops and courses for writers. E-mail: sallyann@sallyannsheridan.com

FURTHER READING

If you wish to learn more about feng shui, Eastern spirituality or the flow of energy throughout the universe, the following books can help you.

Early Chinese Mysticism, Livia Kohn, Princeton University Press 1991

The Field, Lynne McTaggart, Harper Collins 2003

A History of China: Prehistory to c.1800 – vol.1, J.A.G. Roberts, Sutton Publishing 1996

Ki in Daily Life, Koichi Tohei, Japan Publications Trading Co. 1978

Lighting the Eye of the Dragon, Dr Baolin Wu, Macmillan Education Australia 2000

The Little Book of Feng Shui, J.M. Sertori, Dempsey Parr 1999

Safe as Houses? Ill Health and Electro-Stress in the Home, David Cowan and Rodney Girdlestone, Gateway Books 1996

Shinto, Sokyo Ono, Tuttle Publishing 1994

T'ai Chi Journey, John Lash, Element Books 1989

Taoism: Way Beyond Seeking, Alan Watts, HarperCollins 1999

The Taoist Body, Kristofer Schipper (trs. Karen C. Duval), University of California Press 1994

Understanding Reality, Chang Po-Tuan (trs. Thomas Cleary), University of Hawaii Press 1988

INDEX

AUTHOR'S ACKNOWLEDGMENTS

This book would not have been born without the help and support of loads of people, including the following.

Martin Shaw, my dearest friend, who has helped me think things through. He is a wise, spiritual and gentle being; we walk the same pathway!

"Namaste" to my masters, teachers and gurus – Sai Baba, Master Li, Thubten Gyatso, Maitreya and Lillian Too; and to Annie, Kris, Kerry, Sally, Tom, Jodie, Keira, Evelyn and George!

All at dbp for their kindness, care and understanding, especially Bob, fellow bird-watcher, who saw the same vision of the book as I did; Kelly, my Irish Galactic Princess, who made the book sparkle and buzz; and Katie, "Grasshopper", who helped immensely, by asking all the right questions at all the right times.

Everyone who has asked me – by e-mail, by letter, by word of mouth, by phone – about feng shui and how it works. It is for them that this book has been written – to answer their questions.